T0306056

"Calling all social innovators and change makers! *This Little World* provides a pragmatic blueprint for those who want to activate positive change in the world through technology. Halvorson and Kurtz's book is an important contribution to the rapidly developing tech for good industry."

Justin Spelhaug, *Vice President Tech for Social Impact,*
Microsoft

"Halvorson and Kurtz provide clear guidance for tech-enabled social entrepreneurship, with the important message that the human fundamentals matter most."

Kentaro Toyama, Ph.D., *Author of Geek Heresy:*
Rescuing Social Change from the Cult of Technology

"*This Little World* shows tech can be good, when designed responsibly. AI innovation provides new ways to make real progress towards the UN Sustainable Development Goals—and will ultimately support the creation of sustainable and inclusive economies."

Jean-Philippe Courtois, *Executive Vice President and*
President, National Transformation Partnerships, Microsoft

"*This Little World* fills an important strategic gap among leadership and training materials for the growing nonprofit and for-profit marketplace. This book hits the 'sweet spot' by balancing aspirational information about social impact work with the practical skills required to build scalable projects. I strongly recommend this project and its authors."

Julia Roberts, *President and CEO, BRAC USA*

"Must-read, right now."

Ben Jackson, *CEO, Guardify*

"Halvorson and Kurtz are bold, boundless thinkers. *This Little World* is an exciting tool for organizations that are preparing to embrace change and lean into social innovation. Both a practical guide and an inspirational call to action, this book is a masterclass on how institutions can leverage innovation, technology, and change theory to level up their social impact."

Allan Belton, *President, Pacific Lutheran University*

"An engaging and practical introduction to the opportunities and mechanics of social entrepreneurship useful to students in both business and liberal arts settings. This book equips readers to become 'changemakers for good' by combining interdisciplinary thinking, historical understanding, creative and ethical use of technology, and empathetic leadership."

Karen E. Spierling, *Ph.D., Professor of History and Inaugural Director of the Global Commerce Program, Denison University*

"Halvorson and Kurtz's book sheds light on the challenges and critical elements of success associated with creating and scaling technologies that positively serve society."

Luis Salazar, *Founder and CEO, AI4SP*

"*This Little World* is a rare guide for aspiring social innovators."

Morgan Grimm, *Senior Communications Associate, Tala*

"Objective insights that have forced some of the most seasoned experts in the non-profit sector to re-evaluate long-held beliefs."

Chris Emura, *Executive Director, Applied Science & Technology, Allen Institute for AI*

"Kurtz and Halvorson's approach is refreshingly brilliant. Through case study examples and practical instruction, they enable organizations of any size—small business to enterprise, government to nonprofit—to develop a plan that leads to structural, scalable, and sustainable impact through continuous improvement."

Cameron Royce Turner, *Vice President, Data Science, Kin + Carta*

"A must-read for the changemakers working to shape our collective future of limitless potential."

Sam Ushio, *Founder, Ikigai Lab*

"Kurtz possesses a remarkable blend of curiosity, creativity, energy, compassion, drive, and palpable *joie de vivre*. She is the consummate connector of ideas, people, and purpose—and has an uncanny ability to recognize meaning out of unexpected personal relationships and in developing and supporting scalable social impact organizations. Her ability to put this meaning into motion is unparalleled."

Sara Boyd, *Founder, Ascend Advisory LLC*

This Little World

Our planet has never been smaller. Technological advancements have compressed time and space, making the world more immediate and interconnected. *This Little World* clearly sets out how social innovation practices can enable organizations and communities to create a more sustainable, just, and equitable future for our shared lives on Earth.

Today, cloud-based communication systems span the globe, connecting people and markets in the blink of an eye. Remote workers interact daily on high-impact, virtual teams. Telehealth professionals provide medical care to the residents of secluded mountain villages. But a shrinking planet is not without its challenges: climate change, food shortages, pollution, and war are persistent headwinds. We need strategies and tools that promote stability and growth, and we need technology that is more inclusive, trusted, and focused on community goals. *This Little World* seeks to inspire those who aim to explore the rich and rewarding world of social innovation. It is a practical guide to innovation opportunities that will enrich an organization's capacity for transformation and impact. The book explores how social impact employees can create projects that are purpose-driven, scalable, and successful. With insights from leading social innovators, the book demonstrates how "tech for good" organizations are using social innovation strategies, emerging tools, and sustainable practices to support environmental causes, humanitarian initiatives, accessibility, healthcare, cultural heritage, and more.

This Little World: A How-To Guide for Social Innovators is for technologists, business leaders, managers, and employees in the social impact sector, as well as anyone with aspirations for purpose-driven outcomes in their work. Corporate executives, entrepreneurs, and students alike can learn from this new model of innovation, where it is possible to do good and do well.

For more about the This Little World project, visit www.thislittleworld.org.

Michael J. Halvorson, Ph.D., is a professor of business and innovation history at Pacific Lutheran University and the author of 40 books about history, computing, and technology.

Shelly Cano Kurtz is an award-winning social entrepreneur and marketer. She is an advisor for Concordia and on the Board of Directors at Guardify and the Center for Workforce Inclusion.

This Little World

A How-To Guide for Social Innovators

Michael J. Halvorson and Shelly Cano Kurtz

Routledge
Taylor & Francis Group

LONDON AND NEW YORK

Cover design: Willa Rector

First published 2025
by Routledge
4 Park Square, Milton Park, Abingdon, Oxon OX14 4RN

and by Routledge
605 Third Avenue, New York, NY 10158

Routledge is an imprint of the Taylor & Francis Group, an informa business

© 2025 Michael J. Halvorson and Shelly Cano Kurtz

British Library Cataloguing-in-Publication Data
A catalogue record for this book is available from the British Library

ISBN: 978-1-032-73731-7 (hbk)
ISBN: 978-1-032-70892-8 (pbk)
ISBN: 978-1-003-46566-9 (ebk)

DOI: 10.4324/9781003465669

Typeset in Sabon
by codeMantra

Contents

	Acknowledgments	xii
	Foreword by Jeff Raikes and Tricia Raikes	xiv
1	Think Big, Start Small	1
	This Little World	2
	Embrace a Changemaking Mindset	2
	Who We Are	4
	Defining Social Impact	5
	Forestmatic and Sustainable Climate Action	7
	Working with a Shared Sense of Purpose	9
2	Opportunities for Impact	13
	Global Challenges and the Future	14
	Raising Standards of Living	15
	The Social Impact Sector	18
	Rooted in Sustainable Development	20
	Tools for Measuring Success	23
	Identifying Needs in the Community	25
3	Digital Transformation Strategies	29
	Innovating to Protect Children and Enable Justice	30
	Deploying a Cloud-Based Solution	32
	Using Success Metrics	33
	Digital Transformation Frameworks	35
	The Pace of Digitalization	38
	Low-Cost Tools and Infrastructure	40
4	Embedding Purpose into Projects	45
	The Right to Be Understood	46
	Empathy and Compassion	47
	Voiceitt's Speech Recognition Technology	50
	Systemic Funding for Disabilities	52

Finding Your "Why"   56
No Limbits and Shark Tank   57
Immerse Yourself   60

5   Design Thinking for Changemakers   63
    A Human-Centered Approach   63
    Empathy in Design   68
    Capturing Rainwater in West Africa   72
    Defining Your Problem   73
    Ideation for Impact   77
    Civic Engagement in Tacoma   79
    Prototype and Test Scenarios   82

6   Developing a Theory of Change   87
    What's Theory of Change?   88
    Creating a Minimum Viable Product   91
    Technology for the Public Interest   94
    Find Your Ikigai   96
    Equal Opportunity Schools   98
    Agent of Change: Susan Koehler   101
    The Center for Workforce Inclusion   102

7   Data for Social Impact   107
    Success Metrics and Innovation   108
    Social Return on Investment   109
    What Data Should We Collect?   112
    Case Study: An MVP that Measures Impact   114
    Exploring Common Data Models   117
    Guardify's Data Management Strategy   119
    Digital Dashboards   121

8   Scaling for Impact   125
    What Is Scaling?   125
    The 80/20 Rule   128
    Disruptive Innovation   130
    Nine Conditions for Scaling   131
    Scaling Through Creative Partnerships   142

9   AI for Good   147
    The AI for Good Movement   148
    OpenAI and ChatGPT   152

Witty Works: Detecting Unconscious Bias   153
Career Training for Social Impact   155
Fostering Trust   156
AI Integration with Nonprofits   159
Biomonitoring with Bees   160

About the Authors   165
Index   167

Acknowledgments

We're delighted you selected *This Little World* to learn more about social innovation. When we began this book, we had an ambitious goal. We wanted to study and share the best practices of social entrepreneurs, innovators, educators, and industry leaders with deep experience in social impact innovation.

We didn't anticipate the depth or quality of responses we would receive! Over the past three years, we have interviewed hundreds of people, visited numerous agencies and places of business, traveled to conferences and research libraries, and spent a lot of time on email and conference calls. It has been a great pleasure learning from innovators, working with students, hearing stories of success and failure, and comparing notes about best practices.

We can't list everyone, but we'd like to thank the following people who made a real impact on our thinking and shared their hearts and souls with us: Heven Ambachew, Alexander Andino, Erik Arnold, Akhtar Badshah, Shanti Benoit-Boyce, Erik Benson, Sara Boyd, Charlie Bresler, Jeff Calkins, Mary Campbell, Matt Cherry, Erica Cole, Jean-Philippe Courtois, Mattia Curmá, Dusty Davidson, Chris Emura, Nadia Fischer, Taylor Frerichs, Heidi Funston, Alex Gounares, Morgan Grimm, Felix Halvorson, Charles Hammerman, Teresa Huizar, Ben Jackson, Sara Jacobsen, Marcus Knight, Susan Koehler, Brennan LaBrie, Ying Li, Frank McCosker, Gary Officer, Tina Patel, Sasha Rabkin, Jeff Raikes, Tricia Raikes, Willa Rector, Helen Chong Rekers, Julia Roberts, Ana Salazar, Luis Salazar, Rita Santelli, Jackie Schafer, Shelly Smelser, Annette Smith, Sara Smolley, Ali Spain, Justin Spelhaug, Karen Spierling, Kate Steele, Kentaro Toyama, Cameron Turner, Sam Ushio, Victoria Vrana, Valérie Vuillerat, Ed Weber, Danny Weissberg, Christi Wilkins, Vitalii Zakhozhyi, and George Zeno.

At Routledge, we'd like to thank our publisher and production team, including Rebecca Marsh, Lauren Whelan, Cathy Hurren, and Katherine Laidler. The early research and writing of this manuscript took place at Oxford University. Special thanks to St. Anne's

College, Kirsten Jellard, Athena Demetriou, and the staff at the Saïd Business School Library.

Pacific Lutheran University also supplied much support and attention to our project, including essential contributions from Michael Artime, Allan Belton, Joanna Gregson, Sue Loiland, Rebekah Mergenthal, Mark Mulder, and Mike Schleeter. Generous support for teaching Innovation Studies and operating our makerspace came from Dale and Jolita Benson, and Dave and Kendra Uhler.

Of course, our warmest thanks go to our families, who put up with us during the long gestation of this project. Thank you, Kim, Henry, Felix, Nate, Gabi, and Jude. We love you very much!

Foreword

Jeff Raikes and Tricia Raikes

In 2017, Shelly Kurtz walked into our office at the Raikes Foundation for the first time. She was brought in by Luis Salazar, an entrepreneur who we had worked with during our years at Microsoft Corporation. Shelly came to present her go-to-market plan for a new web portal that we were creating based on research from Stanford University, which is known today as Giving Compass. The platform was being built to help individuals inform their charitable giving. We recognized that if people like us were having a hard time sorting through the myriad of web articles and social media messages about nonprofit organizations, other donors could also use some help. Our collective goal was to create a tool that would support and accelerate impact-driven philanthropy. We recognized the need for an accessible resource that would allow people to learn about quality charities, vet organizations, and connect people who share a passion for philanthropy.

Together, we crafted a shared vision of what was possible for the future of philanthropy—using a democratized approach to information gathering from trusted sources, enabled through technology. At the time, the standard tools of philanthropy consisted of PDFs and a handful of industry assessments by charitable advisors. Today, Giving Compass reaches millions of people and has taken the lead in developing AI tools for the philanthropy sector. None of that would have been possible without rethinking how technology can be used as an agent of change in the social impact sector.

Shelly went on to become the Chief Marketing Officer at Giving Compass, and from there, she co-founded Giving Tech Labs, a social impact innovation lab bringing the best practices of the private sector to support innovation for the public good. As board members and partners, we supported Giving Tech Labs while they were building business models and technologies to address pain points for nonprofits and their beneficiaries.

Shelly traveled the country to inspire nonprofit leaders and private foundations to embrace cloud computing technologies and learn about the diverse needs of communities on the ground. In fact, a trip to Nebraska led to the creation of Shelly's third venture with us, VidaNyx (now Guardify). This venture is purpose-built to protect child victims of sexual assault and abuse, using cloud technology to manage digital evidence. You'll learn more about Guardify and how they used tech for good principles to build low-cost, scalable platforms in this book.

What Is Social Innovation?

Social innovation is more than just getting smart people into a room to solve an important problem. It requires new mindsets and a focus on impact that aims to produce better outcomes for all. Back in 2008, the *Stanford Social Innovation Review* declared, "Social entrepreneurship and social enterprise have become popular and positive rallying points for those trying to improve the world, but social innovation is a better vehicle for understanding and creating social change in all of its manifestations."[1]

Around the time we started Giving Compass, we actively funded the movement around public interest technology. There was a nascent initiative called the Public Interest Technology University Network (PIT-UN) catalyzed through the Ford Foundation. This initiative organized academic institutions into cohorts where our grant dollars supported new program development and experiential learning opportunities, and increased access to technological innovation.

We loved the concept but wanted Shelly's help in reimagining the acronym for this work. Unfortunately, "PIT" doesn't exactly have a positive connotation. As a marketer, Shelly took the challenge and Technology for the Public Interest (Tech4PI) was born. A true multi-disciplinary effort, Tech4PI focuses on quantifiable impact with clear key performance indicators (KPIs), technology that supports the business model, and long-lasting impact that improves people's lives.

As funders, the Raikes Foundation was exploring the new frontiers of catalytic philanthropy and recognizing our opportunity to seed change with a high tolerance for risk. This was a departure from traditional grantmaking.

On the academic front, Dr. Michael J. Halvorson and his university colleagues recognized the emerging trend of cross-sector collaboration and the need for higher education to change the playbook about how students are trained for service in the community. Michael helped to create the first interdisciplinary Innovation Studies program on the West Coast in a small liberal arts college in Tacoma, Washington called Pacific Lutheran University. Michael was an early Microsoft employee who had first-hand experience documenting the PC Revolution and developing curriculum that empowered communities. He was selected to lead social innovation programming at the university, building a social impact network that included students, faculty, alumni, and industry partners.

That's where Shelly and Michael's worlds intersected, which you'll learn more about in this book. It's also an example of the world getting *smaller*, focusing on local, interconnected initiatives that take shape and grow. This is one of the meanings of the book's title *This Little World*, a line from a stirring speech in William Shakespeare's play, *Richard II*.

For Jeff and me, there was a time when our world felt very big.

When we were young, the communities we lived in barely had one or two rotary phones per family. As children, we couldn't have imagined the complex data packets that would one day travel the world in milliseconds. In the 1970s, most of the people we knew corresponded through the United States Postal Service.

We grew up 1,700 miles apart from each other's hometowns of Ashland, Nebraska (Jeff) and Seattle, Washington (Tricia). Ashland is a farm town with less than 1,000 homes. Its most notable attribute is being located exactly halfway between Lincoln and Omaha. Seattle is nestled between the Puget Sound and the Cascade mountains, a sprawling metropolis of retail, business, and technology. But in the 1970s, its largest technology company was Boeing, an airplane manufacturer that was soon to experience a major economic downturn.

We grew up in very different places. Yet both of us ended up working for the same relatively unknown microcomputer software company in Bellevue, Washington. At the time, Microsoft had 100 employees in a generic office building near a freeway. Somewhere between company gatherings and corporate events, we connected on a deeper level. We became the first couple to meet at Microsoft and marry. We worked in different departments and had separate responsibilities, but we both got to witness the power of technology to bring people together. We couldn't have predicted the future, but we're very grateful for the front-row seats we had watching the impact that the Information Age has had on the way the world works. We're still on the edge of our chairs, waiting for social impact to be the unifying driver for technological innovation.

The Role of Philanthropy

Today, most of our time is spent in connection with our work as philanthropists. The original translation of philanthropy is "love of humanity." In practice, our philanthropy is often related to giving our time and our voice to support causes that we believe in, including improving youth-serving systems, which includes housing stability for youth and education, resourcing equity and democracy, and impact-driven philanthropy. We are making investments in systems change, and we seek to positively impact generations of young people to come. In our philanthropy, we aren't driven by the traditional "upside" metrics of market investments or financial returns, but we look at the long-term value of social innovation initiatives in communities.

Philanthropy requires trust and an intrinsic belief that big bets fund programs, founders, and organizations that can change the narrative for communities that are historically underserved.

There are many parallels in technology for the public interest. We see the same opportunity for bravery. The examples set forth in *This Little World* demonstrate rewarding opportunities to effect real change at a speed we have never seen before. There is now a convergent space where optimists and solutionists can co-create systems, regardless of industry, geography, or sector expertise.

Today, every company can be a technology company. And every company can have a positive social impact. This book shows you how.

The challenges of our world, from supporting every child to receive a quality education to closing the pay gap, cannot be solved by governments or philanthropists or nonprofits alone. We have the opportunity to create a collective impact when we take a look at the full system. This includes the role of the private sector in developing thoughtful market-led solutions. It also includes academic institutions adapting curricula to teach social innovation in public interest technology. Lastly, it requires the creativity and political will of nonprofit organizations to collaborate and accelerate digital transformation.

In our early career at Microsoft, we saw the PC Revolution unfold before us. The vision of putting a computer on every desk and in every home was largely realized in the developing world. We learned first-hand the power to dream big and work with intentionality. Today, the world has truly never been smaller. We are connected in ways we couldn't have imagined. And yet, with cloud computing and AI, it feels like things are just getting started.

It is our hope that this book helps to inspire the next generation of creators to focus on solutions that matter. The best social innovation requires an entrepreneurial spirit and an interdisciplinary environment, two things that Shelly and Michael know a lot about.

This Little World: A How-To Guide for Social Innovators is a guidebook for leaders and technologists to understand their vital role in building sustainable digital impact tools. It's also for early-career professionals and nonprofit practitioners looking to understand how to turn passion and purpose into social progress at scale. Corporate executives, entrepreneurs, and students alike can learn from this new model of innovation, where it is possible to do good and do well.

There is space for everyone to contribute, from rocket scientists to stay-at-home parents. No one should feel left behind. This book will get you and your organization ready to solve for good. Everyone is welcome into this emerging field.

After all, innovation is not simply about success or accolades. It's about listening, learning, and sharing your insights with others, so that the world and its communities can flourish.

Be bold and start making your journey from inspiration to impact.

Jeff Raikes and Tricia Raikes
Co-Founders, Raikes Foundation

Note

1 James A. Phills Jr., Kriss Deiglmeier, and Dale T. Miller, "Rediscovering Social Innovation," *Stanford Social Innovation Review* 6, no. 4 (2008): 34–43. https://ssir.org/articles/entry/rediscovering_social_innovation. Accessed December 15, 2023.

1 Think Big, Start Small

This book is written to build excitement for social innovation in organizations and communities that want to create a more sustainable, just, and equitable future for our planet.

Whether you do this work now or are considering a future career, this roadmap is for you!

Our inspiration for *This Little World* came from conversations with hundreds of employees who are working in social impact organizations or who are preparing to do so. Many are Millennials or members of so-called Generation Z. Others have been part of the wave of Big Tech layoffs that hit the industry in 2023 and 2024. In conversation after conversation, we've learned the same fundamental lesson: Workers are ready for something *new*. They want purpose-driven jobs in our economy that offer financial stability *and* contribute to just and sustainable communities. Employees want to be creative *and* pursue careers that support their values.

When we looked into these goals a little deeper, we recognized that purpose-driven employment is really an aspiration for *every* demographic of the workforce. By "purpose-driven," we mean labor or business activity that is defined as *socially beneficial* or which *contributes to the greater good of society*. This value-based expectation is now articulated by the world's largest corporations. Satya Nadella, CEO of Microsoft, speaks to meaning and purpose in this way: "The purpose of a corporation is to create profitable solutions to the challenges of people and planet—in every community and every country. This is what our customers, partners, and colleagues expect, and it's what the world demands from today's corporations."[1]

As technologists and entrepreneurs, our vision is also to create viable and sustainable solutions to the world's most pressing problems. We seek to empower students, social innovators, impact investors, philanthropists, engineers, and community partners to create technology for the public interest that addresses urgent social and environmental needs. The time has never been better to pursue purpose-driven work through creative partnerships, businesses, and social impact organizations.

DOI: 10.4324/9781003465669-1

This Little World

The title of our book comes from a well-known passage of William Shakespeare's play *Richard II*:

> This royal throne of kings, this scepter'd isle,
> This earth of majesty...
> This happy breed of men, *this little world*,
> This precious stone set in the silver sea...[2]

The speaker of these words is an aging statesman who expresses love for his country and its people. But he's also worried about clouds he sees on the horizon. Although the realm is buzzing with potential, it's also threatened by internal and external forces. Under siege, his world feels small, precious, and fragile.

We understand the sentiment. Despite daily reports of innovation and achievement in our own time, planet Earth feels *smaller* not larger.

Cloud-based communication systems span the globe, connecting people and markets in the blink of an eye. Remote workers interact daily via virtual teams. Telehealth specialists provide support to the residents of secluded villages.

Each new advancement compresses time and space, making our world more immediate and interconnected. A compelling digital product or campaign can now achieve worldwide distribution in a matter of weeks—or less.

But the shrinking world is not without its challenges. Population growth, industrialization, and war have made the Earth more fragile. Climate change, food shortages, and pollution are persistent headwinds.

Our little, precious world needs strategies that promote stability and growth. We need technological innovation that is inclusive, trusted, and focused on community goals. Each action or intent, however small, can have immense impact.

Embrace a Changemaking Mindset

This Little World explores an emerging consensus about how social innovation practices and technological innovation can improve lives, protect the Earth, and promote prosperity. We want to think big, start small, and scale for impact. The future of our planet is at stake.

Embedding purpose into products has moved from the margins of corporate activity to be an urgent *expectation* for employees, managers, customers, and stakeholders. The social impact sector is built around this vision for changemaking, where *social and environmental issues are creatively addressed, economic growth is inclusive, technical systems are trusted,* and *the fundamental rights of people are unequivocally supported.*[3] This focus on change seeks to upset the status quo by recognizing that traditional business activity has often supported favored or select groups, producing goods and services that are expensive, unsustainable, and designed primarily for the benefit of one group of people.

What types of social innovation projects fit this description, and what skills are necessary for the employees that design and implement them? Which emerging technologies can be harnessed to do this work? What are the creative mindsets that shape successful nonprofit, for-profit, and government-affiliated social impact organizations? And on the economic front: What types of investments will *really* help your organization address practical problems and achieve a positive return on investment (ROI)?

We wrote this book to address these questions because we've noticed a lack of resources designed to support new social impact projects and teams, especially in the tech sector. Despite a period of rapid growth and investment in the industry, much of the learning that takes place in social innovation is still through paid consultants, high-priced workshops, and specialty websites. Few universities or postsecondary institutions offer curriculum to support social impact training. Within the industry, an emphasis on "digital transformation" has raised awareness about the need for new technology, but not on which systems to select or how to integrate them.

Moreover, the core business activities in a social enterprise are typically structured *differently* than in traditional corporations. For example, tech for good startups are often determined to create value *rapidly*, moving from design to prototype to scaling in a progression that seems bewildering to conventional administrators. In terms of work style, tech for good companies often prefer remote work and virtual interaction, developing learning pathways around social media networks, webinars, and professional tools like Zoom or LinkedIn.

Measurement and teaming have also taken the spotlight in social impact organizations. Social entrepreneurs use key performance indicators (KPIs) to evaluate core business activities, and they curate rich data sources to identify trends and make decisions. They seek regular input from social impact partners, foundations, and community members. Equity and inclusion have also gained urgency in social impact work, a welcome transformation that is strengthening all sectors of the industry. When social entrepreneurs search for employees to do innovation work, it's just as important to recruit for moral fiber, empathy, and cross-cultural experiences as it is for traditional business or technology skills.

This Little World explores each of these social innovation roles and mindsets through rich case studies taken from local, regional, and global social impact organizations. Each chapter aims to teach tangible skills to changemakers who aspire to deliver social impact, particularly those who are curious about how digital transformation and tech for good strategies are revolutionizing the field. We're optimistic about the future and see each opportunity for social innovation as a chance to learn and build community solutions with fascinating partners. We hope that you agree!

Who We Are

Michael Halvorson and Shelly Cano Kurtz are two experienced social impact practitioners with a passion for social innovation and many years of experience in the tech for good landscape. We both live in the Pacific Northwest and are alumni of the same school, Pacific Lutheran University (PLU) in Tacoma, Washington. Our interest in impact work grew out of our early grounding in Lutheran higher education and the belief that creative social engagement and service are essential parts of citizenship and professional life. Although we have both spent time in technology-oriented companies, our personal and professional experiences are unique, and we hope that this mixture serves you well.

Shelly Cano Kurtz is a social entrepreneur and consultant who has founded numerous social innovation organizations, including a social impact incubator, an evidence management solution, and a data insights platform for entrepreneurs. Shelly is also an advisor for Concordia, a bipartisan organization dedicated to building cross-sector partnerships, and the Center for Workforce Inclusion, a nonprofit focused on workforce development for older Americans. She has been involved in over 200 go-to-market campaigns and regularly serves as a mentor for social innovators in the U.S.

Michael Halvorson, Ph.D., is a professor of business history and innovation who writes and teaches about digital transformation and public interest technology. He was an early employee at Microsoft, contributing to the development of Microsoft Press, Visual Studio, and Microsoft Office. He is currently director of Innovation Studies at PLU, an interdisciplinary program that emphasizes collaborative problem solving, human-centered design, and social entrepreneurship. He is the author of 40 books about history and technology, and served for ten years as an executive leader at Compass Housing Alliance, a social impact organization in Seattle.

Together, the authors are able to share industry experience and insider knowledge about a sector of the U.S. economy that currently receives over $2.8 trillion of annual revenue in the U.S. They present insights and case studies from many of the organizations that they have worked with, including Microsoft, the Bill & Melinda Gates Foundation, Guardify (formerly VidaNyx), the City of Tacoma, and Pacific Lutheran University. They draw research data from over 500 academic studies and more than 3,000 tech for good organizations that are using emerging technology to address social and environmental challenges.

Defining Social Impact

As we get started, let's begin with a definition of what social impact is and who is invited to do this work. (Hint: The answer to the second question is "Everyone!")

At its core, the term "social impact" refers to improving the well-being of individuals and communities by addressing social and economic issues such as poverty, inequality, access to education, and healthcare. This type of work can be done by individuals, nonprofit organizations, government entities, and for-profit corporations. Social impact work can also take a range of forms, including community development initiatives, advocacy, philanthropy, entrepreneurship, social innovation projects, and other activities. In each of these contexts, the goal of social impact is to create positive change in society through actions that address the root causes of social problems.

Social impact practitioners are people who are committed to enacting these changes through jobs or other roles in the social impact sector. These positions include policy analyst, community organizer, program manager, social impact investor, software engineer, scientist, designer, technical worker, data analyst, corporate social responsibility officer, digital marketing specialist, and a range of employees who perform traditional business functions.

Although social impact practitioners have traditionally been associated with the *nonprofit sector* (organizations such as food banks, homeless shelters, or the Special Olympics), today all manner of educational institutions, for-profit corporations, nonprofits, and government entities have staff members that are actively engaged in social impact activity. In some cases, these changemakers break away from existing organizations and create something entirely *new*. When this happens, we often refer to them as *social innovators*, *social entrepreneurs*, or *impact entrepreneurs*, especially when their work leads to systemic social change or new social movements.[4] (On LinkedIn, Michael and Shelly are both members of the group *Impact Entrepreneurs*, which currently has over 38,000 members interested in systemic changemaking.) Social impact work does not just feature new enterprises or grassroots initiatives that are connected to current events. The agents for social change can also work from *within* an existing organization to rejuvenate its mission or its goals. This type of innovator is often referred to as an *intrapreneur* (or corporate entrepreneur), to highlight their creative role inside an existing corporation or entity.

Since the widespread deployment of computing and technology infrastructures, many social impact advocates have placed big bets on *technological innovation* as a catalyst to promote meaningful change in society. A belief in the promise of scalable technology for the public good is often referred to as *tech for good* or the *tech for good movement*, because it envisions the constructive, amplifying effect of technology for all people when digital systems are thoughtfully designed and equitably distributed. Shelly co-founded X4i.org as a tech directory and learning lab to nourish this type of thinking, because tech for good businesses often take similar approaches to digital transformation and emerging technology.

This Little World evaluates numerous tech for good organizations because they approach social challenges through community building, knowledge sharing, and collective impact models. But the authors of this book are also aware of the unintended consequences of technological innovation. The important book *Geek Heresy: Rescuing Social Change from the Cult of Technology*, by Kentaro Toyama, soberly discusses the ways that technological innovation has often fallen short in addressing social ills.[5] We appreciate the lessons in this publication. Like Toyama, we hope to offer a balanced approach to digital transformation that is guided by recent research, clear objectives, and results that can be measured. As part of the preparation for this book, we met with hundreds of social impact practitioners to compare notes about digital transformation and social innovation. Several chapters in this book have their roots in the curriculum that Michael uses when he teaches social innovation to college students and community members.

Clearly, curriculum and technology alone can't address every social ill or human shortcoming. But it is reasonable to believe that compassionate people working together can genuinely advance the public good by using innovative thinking, education, and appropriate technical systems. The core commitments of this work should include expanding human agency, fostering accountability, working for justice, and protecting the planet.

Said a different way, *we believe that working to improve the lives of others is not just a vocation for teachers, do-gooders, or idealists.* Doing good for the planet is a way to lead an extraordinary life, where you take your personal story, resources, and sense of vocation and share them with others to build a legacy for the future.

This moment calls for change and renewal. If you aspire to a purpose-driven career, know this: This little world needs *you.* There are thousands of opportunities in the for-profit, nonprofit, and social impact sector for a wide range of workers who want to tackle the world's most challenging problems. A large talent pool is shifting to the social impact sector now, and we expect to see thousands of startups in the coming years that promote meaningful change and work to improve the lives of others. The time is *now!*

Forestmatic and Sustainable Climate Action

To share our excitement about the social impact movement, we conclude this chapter with a case study about Forestmatic (www.forestmatic.com), a purpose-driven organization that Shelly consulted with as they were developing their go-to-market strategy in the U.S. Forestmatic exemplifies how a small team of relatively inexperienced innovators has been able to take their passion for sustainable climate action and turn it into a social enterprise that uses technology in a creative way. This is their story, and it provides a sample of the rich case studies that will be featured in this book.

In 2020, Tarek Ayoub, Mattia Curmà, and Alexander Verresen became interested in tree planting as a way to address global climate change.

Relatively inexperienced in the tactics of social innovation, the three graduate students met in a capstone course in Madrid to study social and environmental problems. Like most advanced college courses, the class had a solid analytical framework and encouraged students to pick a global challenge and study its underlying causes and potential solutions. The team selected climate change and began to research *reforestation* as a strategy to engage both businesses and communities in sustainability. Not only did reforestation help to trap carbon dioxide (CO_2) in trees, but it had been proven to unite neighborhoods and restore biodiversity to natural landscapes.

When Tarek, Mattia, and Alexander studied reforestation, they learned that most of the work done to plant trees was relatively haphazard when looked at globally. Despite the proliferation of technical tools that enabled the collection, storage, and analysis of data, no one had applied this technology to reforestation campaigns. When local businesses advertised that they were supporting reforestation to offset CO_2, there was no way to verify that this work had been accomplished, or for consumers to track the progress of individual tree-planting campaigns. Reforestation seemed remote and disconnected from everyday life.

Although they were not prepared to start a social impact organization, Tarek, Mattia, and Alexander used their capstone to explore the benefits of tree planting, and they started discussing the issue with reforestation experts. Moving beyond the constraints of a typical grad school project, they also sought input from both technologists and members of the communities that were hardest hit by forest removal. During the process, Mattia also connected with Shelly and her team, who had recently started an incubator project to track and support new tech for good companies. Forestmatic was invited to be featured in the X4i.org tech directory because they had used innovative data related to reforestation, and they utilized a cloud-based solution that displayed "live" data about tree planting from around the globe.

Within a few months, the team expanded to include additional advisors with the skills necessary to build tracking tools that could aggregate and display reforestation data. Additional research helped the students discover that over 50 regional and international agencies were engaged with tree-planting efforts, and that the United Nations had addressed reforestation in its Sustainable Development Goals (SDGs), specifically SDG #13: Climate Action and SDG #15: Life on Land. By connecting to existing initiatives and discovering the role that they could play in a collaborative solution, the team learned how to complement the work of others. Tarek, Mattia, and Alexander believed that regular citizens *and* the leaders of local businesses would support tree planting as a "green solution" if it seemed more tangible and verifiable.

By late 2020, the students' professor, Marcos Eguillor, recognized the progress that they were making, and advised the team to consider founding a for-profit social impact organization to bring to market the tool that they had designed. As an expression of confidence in their prototype, Professor Eguillor also became a financial investor and promoted their work through his personal and professional networks.

In November 2020, the group officially founded Forestmatic, a digital platform that allowed global tree-planting projects to be trackable, traceable, and transparent with up-to-the-minute data worldwide. Using a graphical website and tree-planting "dashboard," any user could follow the progress of reforestation initiatives, down to the individual tree. Businesses that supported tree planting to offset their carbon footprint could also prove to their stakeholders that planting actions were *actually* taking place, because the information was available on a published website with graphical tools and visualizers.

Within a year, Forestmatic announced that over four million trees had been planted by partner organizations, and each tree could be tracked using their digital tracking technology. The reforestation data was available for five continents, and it demonstrated that over 500,000 tons of carbon had been sequestered, mitigating global warming in a tangible way. It was only the beginning, but just two years after brainstorming in a college seminar, the Forestmatic team had released a successful purpose-driven product. The social business reflected their values and commitments, and engaged with a community of like-minded partners. Later that year, they received recognition from the United Nations as a top "green solution" provider, contributing tangibly to the SDGs.

Working with a Shared Sense of Purpose

Forestmatic is just one of many social impact organizations that have used scalable digital tools to promote environmentally beneficial interventions in our world. Their journey from idea to product was not overly complex from an engineering point of view, but it did involve new ways of creating value that deserve careful study. We'll introduce the strategies needed to achieve this type of impact in future chapters, but at this point it is useful to comment on a few of the leadership principles that the Forestmatic team followed when they began.

The first is that the Forestmatic organization remains small. As they complete their second year of business activity in 2023, the company still lists just six employees on their website. The three founders (Tarek, Mattia, and Alexander) continue to focus on day-to-day operations, building their business and interacting with potential customers and partners. The main objectives for the team are enhancing the Forestmatic application and raising funds for expansion. Like any for-profit business, they need to produce a viable product and cover their operating expenses until sufficient revenues arrive to pay operational costs and other bills. But it is important to see how they have already *scaled their ideas*, rather than the footprint of their organization. Forestmatic was committed to *changemaking*, not simply profitability. They have added employees only when they believed it would enhance their *impact*.

Second, the training and background of each employee is fascinating. Their international training and experience has made global collaboration possible, and each worker brought the skills to manage a range of complex tasks.

Alexander Verresen had a background in entrepreneurship and digital transformation, and he took the role of CEO for the company. Alexander lives in Portugal and maintains overall responsibility for the company's business operations. But Alexander is also a jack-of-all-trades, writing in a recent profile that he learned the HTML and CSS coding protocols so that he could enhance the company's website.

Mattia Curmà also has a broad, interdisciplinary background in business development, art and design, video production, and media writing. He lives in Italy and learned the Python programming language to improve Forestmatic's core software product. When needed, he is also a regular blogger for the company.

Tarek Ayoub is fluent in Arabic, French, and English and lives in Mexico City, although he completed his first entrepreneurial work in Lebanon. Tarek focuses on attracting new business partners and establishing global relationships, a task he is especially well prepared for.

Rounding out the staff positions, Forestmatic employs a marketing and digital content specialist (who lives in Portugal), a part-time technology advisor (who lives in Brazil), and an unpaid mentor/investor (who lives in Spain). The team works 100 percent remotely, with a corporate address in Brussels.

In this tech for good company, each of the job descriptions is "fuzzy" and overlaps considerably with others. The employees pitch in as needed to meet company goals. In management-speak, we would describe this arrangement as a "flat" hierarchy, where everyone contributes and works daily on the company mission.

Most of Forestmatic's employees are new to social impact work, so there is little experience on the team with sustainability initiatives or so-called "green solutions." The founders' desire to do purpose-driven work motivated them to study a global challenge and build professional relationships to address it. Gradually, they have learned more about sustainability as they have interacted with partners who share similar goals.

Another noteworthy trend is that each member of the team has contributed to digital content creation in some way, often learning new skills to do the work. A familiarity with data collection and analysis permeates the organization, and most team members are willing to assist with software or media creation. They work remotely and seem to like doing so. If anything, a virtual office arrangement seems to fuel their curiosity for learning and problem solving. It also reduces costs, because they don't have a large corporate office to pay for.

Finally, it is obvious that the Forestmatic team has been strongly influenced by a seminar in social innovation principles and the inspiration of several thoughtful mentors. They learned key social entrepreneurship techniques, which helped them design a purpose-driven product using the appropriate cloud-based technology. This process inspired trust with their customers and helped them address new and untapped markets. A shared sense of purpose continually drives the team forward.

The social impact sector is large and growing rapidly, with innovative companies like Forestmatic coming to market on a weekly basis. In the U.S. alone, spending on social impact-related projects has reached an estimated $2.8 trillion per year and involves over 1.9 million social impact organizations. Large technology companies like Microsoft are sensing the opportunity, and they are designing platforms and services specifically for social impact organizations. As tech companies prepare services for social impact groups, they also provide technical training programs or "skilling" curricula, so that a new wave of workers can enter the social impact field. Globally, the market opportunity to address the UN SDGs has reached approximately $12 trillion per year.

As large as this social impact opportunity is, there are relatively few software tools to analyze and coordinate activities in the sector. Moreover, there are few training pathways into social innovation careers, especially the tech for good jobs that involve social innovation strategies and emerging technology like artificial intelligence (AI). This leads us back to our core question: *What are the skills and mindsets needed to be a changemaker?*

Social innovators need essential business and communication skills, a desire to collaborate with partners and community members, and a willingness to experiment with data and technical systems. A hybrid set of skills seems to be the common denominator in most tech for good organizations. Social innovators also need to understand the problems and worldviews of others, and meet their clients where they are. From empathy and compassion come the best insights to critique existing systems and design initiatives that truly support human flourishing.

In *This Little World*, we offer numerous pathways into this way of thinking, including step-by-step materials that explore how successful organizations inspire innovation and foster creativity. As part of our journey, we'll explore effective digital transformation strategies, how to embed purpose into projects, and the power of inclusive, human-centered design. We'll also discuss best practices for managing data, how to develop a theory of change, and how to design projects so that they can deliver social impact at scale. When you need to develop specific skills, such as data management techniques, we'll point you in the right direction. In the next chapter, we begin by discussing how social innovators can use the UN SDGs to identify needs and create solutions that address social and environmental challenges.

Notes

1 For Satya Nadella's quote and more about Microsoft's vision for purpose-driven work, see Microsoft Corporation, "Embrace a Changemaking Culture: Where Purpose Meets Impact" (Redmond: WA, 2020), 2.
2 William Shakespeare, *Richard II: The Oxford Shakespeare* (Oxford: Oxford University Press, 2011), 2.1.40.
3 The term "changemaking" has been popularized by Ashoka, a nonprofit organization that has spent decades working with social enterprises. To learn more about their creative programming and materials, visit www.ashoka.org.
4 For helpful definitions of social entrepreneurship and how the phenomenon is being studied in academic circles, see Paul C. Light, *The Search for Social Entrepreneurship* (Washington, DC: Brookings Institution Press, 2008), 1–29.
5 Kentaro Toyama, *Geek Heresy: Rescuing Social Change from the Cult of Technology* (New York: PublicAffairs, 2015).

2 Opportunities for Impact

Our complex, beautiful world is facing many challenges. The Earth's population recently surpassed 8 billion souls and continues to rise. War, pollution, and economic uncertainty are regular headwinds, and so are food shortages, human rights abuses, and a lack of access to basic services like education and healthcare.

It's easy to feel discouraged in the face of problems like this.

But you *can* make a difference. You can do so through individual action, and by partnering with others in communities, businesses, and schools.

This chapter explores purpose-driven work in social impact organizations, a $2.8 trillion segment of the U.S. economy made up of for-profit businesses, nonprofits, and charitable foundations committed to social and environmental causes. We'll sample a range of social impact projects that have improved lives, protected the planet, and promoted growth and prosperity. In particular, we'll see how tech for good firms have pursued changemaking using social innovation strategies and scalable digital tools.

We start by reviewing some of the first attempts to use technology to raise living standards in industrialized nations. Then we'll discuss how similar strategies are being used by modern corporations to tackle global challenges like climate change, poverty, and protecting vulnerable populations.

One of our main claims is that addressing social problems at scale involves *collective action*. To introduce this concept, we'll examine how the United Nations Sustainable Development Goals (UN SDGs) have helped many organizations clarify their ambitions and collaborate with community partners. Our featured case study investigates the Giving Compass Insights tech directory, a data analysis tool that presents comprehensive information about tech for good companies and opportunities in the social impact sector.

DOI: 10.4324/9781003465669-2

Global Challenges and the Future

As we begin, it's useful to be realistic about the times we are living in. We can't address the world's social and environmental challenges unless we acknowledge the problems we're facing.

The 2020s began with a series of overlapping health, environmental, political, and financial crises, each of which has reshaped our economy and global relationships.

The coronavirus pandemic touched every corner of the globe and redefined how healthcare is delivered. Global warming and weather crises have gained momentum and made it clear how fragile our planet is. The war in Ukraine and other conflicts have dramatically increased food shortages, the energy crisis, and housing insecurity. A wave of layoffs at Big Tech companies has created financial strain and worry about careers and the future of work. According to the United Nations, approximately two billion people live in countries that are currently impacted by military conflict.[1]

The resulting uncertainty has impacted financial markets, businesses, and individual lives. Despite numerous political and cultural achievements in our world, every day millions of people still suffer from hunger, poverty, job insecurity, and violence. Homelessness, mental illness, and drug addiction have also become endemic. The gap between rich and poor has never been greater.

What the headlines don't emphasize, however, is that there is also a lot of *progress* taking place in the effort to bring social and economic stability to our communities.

Central to this effort are thousands of social impact organizations that address urgent global issues such as poverty, climate change, peacemaking, access to education, improvements to healthcare, and more. Governments, foundations, corporations, schools, and citizen groups are committing major resources to this work.

Finding the light at the end of the tunnel and productive strategies to get there are the foci of this book. An important principle to begin with is that *you're never alone when you embrace a culture of changemaking for the public good.*

Creative human beings have a long track record of working together to solve social and environmental problems. Over the past century, one of the biggest levers in this work has been investment in *public access technology.* In the late nineteenth and early twentieth centuries, for example, far-reaching investments in scientific research and community infrastructure laid the groundwork for many social and economic improvements around the world.

The success of these projects goes a long way to explaining why social entrepreneurs are so optimistic about the power of technology to promote positive change today. They often lead with the question: "Is there a way that we can use innovation and technology appropriately to support the formation of a just, equitable, and prosperous society?"

We also like this question, and we believe the answer is "yes!"

Before we explain how, though, it's time for an admission: Michael Halvorson is a History professor, and he believes that historical reflection is a great way to find inspiration for social impact projects. Whenever we discuss the potential benefits of public interest technology, he gets a little twinkle in his eye. And he tells a story about a constellation of public access investments a century ago, when new discoveries brought radical changes to the way that people lived. The echoes of that outpouring are still with us.

Enjoy the short digression—it explains the American enchantment with technological innovation and the rise of social impact organizations.

Raising Standards of Living

In the 1870s and 1880s, few Americans had access to clean water, electricity, transportation, or long-distance communication.

This meant that regular people didn't have indoor plumbing, refrigerators, washing machines, automobiles, radios, or telephones. Modern luxuries like airplanes, computers, televisions, and the Internet were distant dreams.

Food spoiled quickly, and basic sanitation was a daily challenge. People walked most of the time, and information traveled slowly. Daily life was much as it had been in the decades before the American Civil War. In terms of public health, it was the era of smallpox, cholera, tuberculosis, measles, and rabies.

One by one, however, a series of technological innovations changed life in the U.S. and most of the world's industrialized nations. Between 1870 and 1970, there was a century-long outpouring of technology, in which a series of public infrastructure projects brought economic growth and prosperity to thousands of global communities.

Scientific experiments with magnetism and electricity led to the widespread deployment of the telegraph (1850s), the telephone (1880s), radio (1920s), and television (1950s). These communication technologies had a revolutionary impact on the quality of people's lives, bringing news, financial data, transportation schedules, and information about new products to millions of people.

At the same time, innovative indoor plumbing systems brought clean water into people's homes, businesses, and tenement buildings.

Across the country, plumbing infrastructures were gradually expanded to include sewer systems and purification plants. By the early 1920s, the availability of clean water and sanitation had a major influence on public health and life expectancy in America. Soon typhoid fever, tuberculosis, diphtheria, and scarlet fever were on the run.

Vaccine development and antibiotic research soon gained momentum, improving the lives of infants and children. Young people survived into adulthood in greater numbers than ever before.

But there was more.

Automobiles and busses took the scene in the 1910s and 1920s, followed by a network of roads, service stations, oil refineries, automobile plants, and car showrooms. Innovative electric devices such as lights, sewing machines, washing machines, refrigerators, and power tools significantly reduced the time needed to prepare food, manage chores, and repair equipment. The time saved allowed citizens to devote attention to other tasks, such as education, hobbies, volunteer work, and entrepreneurial interests.

Why did the technology surge take place?

The source of innovation was *scientific research*, fostered in large part by emerging universities in countries such as the United States, Great Britain, and Germany. Major discoveries in electromagnetism, chemistry, and medicine were turned into social improvements by a creative combination of private investment and government spending on public infrastructure. Collective action by corporations, social entrepreneurs, and the government improved the lives of millions of people.

A Flood of Inventions

When economic historians evaluate this period in history, they describe the technology surge as a singular period of growth that has not been equaled since. In the words of Robert J. Gordon, author of *The Rise and Fall of American Growth*, "The flood of inventions that followed the Civil War utterly transformed life [in America], transferring human attention and energy from the mundane to soaring skyscrapers and airplanes."[2] The average life expectancy in the U.S. jumped from 45 years in 1870 to 72 years in 1970. Real gross domestic product (GDP) per capita increased by a similar rate, as did virtually *all* measures associated with labor productivity and standards of living.

The U.S. was not alone in this expansion—similar public health and infrastructure improvements were realized in Western Europe,

Scandinavia, Japan, Canada, and Australia. The stunning swiftness of the transformation has made Gordon and others wonder if future economic growth can *ever* happen again in this way. In fact, after the 1970s, the global development project for many practitioners has been to bring the rest of the world up to the living and life expectancy gains produced by the first century of growth in industrialized nations.

Understanding the Pattern

Why does this short story about the history of technology matter?

One important takeaway is that funding for scientific research and technological innovation can be a powerful force for good in society. During the early twentieth century, government and private sector funding led to technological innovation that totally transformed the housing, transportation, communication, education, entertainment, and healthcare sectors of the U.S. economy. As factories were electrified, the process created *entirely new jobs* for average people at the same time that it created *entirely new appliances* for them. In other words, the innovation surge benefited workers and consumers alike.[3]

However, despite the boost in life expectancy and living standards, not everyone benefited from the new systems equally. In the U.S., the boom and bust cycles of innovation and investment created *gaps* that needed to be addressed by social institutions and citizens working together in communities. Urban areas generally received more infrastructure improvements than rural areas. Marginalized groups often received limited access to quality housing, transportation, and communication enhancements like local telegraph or telephone stations.[4] Although technological innovation promoted meaningful change in society, it was often left to community organizations to distribute resources equitably, or pitch in when neglected populations were left behind.

To address the gaps, new charitable institutions arrived in the wake of public infrastructure changes. Many of these organizations were promoted by civic or religious groups, such as the Lutheran Sailors and Loggers Mission of Seattle, organized in 1920 to help homeless lumberjacks and dock workers find shelter. Under a new name, Compass Housing Alliance still provides support services in the Seattle area for displaced workers, expanding its offerings as the region has become a major metropolitan area. Despite a century of technological advancement, there are still members of the community who need retraining and support. For many, the outpouring of technological innovation seems exclusionary, widening the gap between rich and poor.

Throughout the twentieth century, thousands of nonprofit organizations fanned out across the United States, caring for the sick, providing healthcare, and working to enable social and educational reform. Their influence can be seen in the rise of food safety laws, immunization programs, public hospitals, schools, and programs to support workers displaced by changes in society.

Several of the first nonprofits spread their influence beyond the U.S., spanning the globe with their advocacy and resources. Examples include the Peabody Education Fund, the Red Cross, the YMCA, the Salvation Army, and the United Way. We now use the comprehensive term "social impact organization" to describe the work that these groups do to address social, environmental, and economic issues. As noted in Chapter 1, social impact work can take a range of forms, including individual support, community development initiatives, political advocacy, philanthropy, education, scientific research, and business activity. In each of these contexts, the goal of social impact work is to create positive change in society through actions that address the root causes of social and environmental problems.

The Social Impact Sector

Today, the social impact sector in the U.S. has become a sophisticated network of charitable, benevolent, and for-profit organizations. It includes one million active charities, 1.7 million businesses, and annual revenues of approximately $2.8 trillion. Nonprofit organizations are still a major part of this work. In fact, according to the World Bank, the U.S. nonprofit sector would be the world's tenth largest economy if it were ranked separately by GDP.

Regardless of the business model, the social impact sector is built around a vision for *changemaking*, or taking creative action to solve social and environmental problems. The sector is a space where global issues are addressed, economic growth is inclusive, and the fundamental rights of people are supported. Some organizations are large, with over 1,000 employees and a multinational organization that spans the globe. Others are small, with one small office and the characteristics of an entrepreneurial startup.

The size of the social impact sector is large enough that it is attracting a wide range of economic partnerships and resources. It draws the attention of citizen groups, corporations, educational institutions, and government entities.

For example, many U.S. corporations have realized that social impact organizations are potential customers for purpose-driven brands and products. Microsoft's Tech for Social Impact group has established a network of 70,000+ social impact organizations that it regularly partners with to pursue its strategic goals. These objectives include supporting inclusive economies, protecting human rights, building organizational trust, and pursuing sustainability initiatives. The company has designed software systems and training resources specifically for social impact organizations, so that they can store information securely in the cloud, manage volunteers, track donors and grants, and more.

The stereotype that social impact organizations are relatively unsophisticated in terms of technology is no longer true, if it ever was. Digital transformation has reconfigured the social impact sector, turning most social impact organizations into *technology companies*, meaning that tech tools and procedures flow organically through their systems. These organizations use computers, data, and management strategies in a similar way that for-profit businesses do.

However, a new type of social impact company has emerged over the last decade that uses technology and resources in a new way. The term "tech for good" has popularized these social enterprises, which generally aim to produce socially beneficial solutions by using social innovation principles and rapidly *scaling* their impact via emerging technology. The tools and techniques that they use include design thinking, Agile methods, cloud computing, artificial intelligence, data analytics, and other emerging systems.

Rapid scaling means *quantitatively increasing the value of a social innovation for the public good*. In addition to quantitative metrics, these firms tend to apply adaptive, learning-oriented approaches to social impact work that are highly influenced by iterative cycles of designing, prototyping, and testing to build value. The characteristics of these organizations are so unique that we highlight several of their management and innovation practices in this book.

Tech for good organizations have the potential to renew society in dramatic ways, similar to the radical gains achieved by the technology "surge" of the late nineteenth and early twentieth centuries. We also believe that human-centered design and a focus on equity and inclusion can help social impact organizations avoid many of the imbalances produced during earlier periods of technological innovation. The future of our planet depends on thoughtful reflection about how to deliver economic growth and innovation so that more people and places can benefit from it.

Rooted in Sustainable Development

What are some of the characteristics of tech for good organizations and how do they support social and environmental flourishing?

Let's start with a few basic statistics.

In late 2022, there were approximately 10,000 self-identified tech for good companies in the United States. A detailed report analyzing this group found that two-thirds of the companies in this category preferred for-profit business models, and just one-third filed for 501(c)(3) "nonprofit" status with the U.S. government.[5]

Ninety percent of tech for good firms generated revenue via the sales of a *product* in 2022, and most of them operated with a business-to-business (B2B) model. This means that the companies worked to address social and environmental needs by supporting other organizations. Tech for good firms have also been significant revenue generators. Seventy-five percent of the 10,000 enterprises surveyed earned $10 million or more during 2022.[6]

In terms of assessment measures, the majority of tech for good firms have adopted the UN SDGs as the preferred "yardstick" or accountability framework to publicize and evaluate their initiatives. Although the UN SDGs were initially adopted by government agencies to assess how much social benefit their investments were producing in international contexts, many North American and European organizations now use them to track domestic goals. Although the SDGs are a defining characteristic of tech for good firms, they are still relatively unfamiliar to many U.S. audiences. For this reason, we'll make regular use of them as we explain how value is created, assessed, and reported by social impact organizations.

What Are the UN SDGs?

In 2015, the leaders of 193 countries gathered at the United Nations to consider a comprehensive development plan featuring 17 interlinked objectives "for people, planet and prosperity."[7] The problems addressed at the global summit were dire and systemic, including food shortages, wars and global conflicts, energy problems, humanitarian concerns, refugee crises, climate change, and environmental degradation. By working collectively on a list of priorities, however, the group hoped to create a set of practical objectives that could benefit not just the richest, most industrialized nations (the beneficiaries of the first technology surge), but all of the nations on Earth.

The result was a shared agenda called the UN Sustainable Development Goals, which aimed to end poverty, protect the planet, and promote well-being and prosperity for all. Seventeen specific goals were announced, and each goal has been further clarified by a selection of *targets and indicators*. Many of the goals were intentionally interrelated, so that they could be used to collectively track progress at national, regional, and local levels. The plan is to encourage political change and investment that spurs innovation and business development, while also monitoring progress and addressing the needs of real people (not just corporations). The target date for achieving the goals has been set ambitiously for 2030.

Since 2015, the UN SDGs have been widely adopted by industry consortia, scientific organizations, governments, international agencies, citizens groups, and more. A major benefit of using the SDGs is that they are not national goals, related to just one government or election cycle, but *global goals*, designed for the benefit of all. Each goal is designed to be supported by a rich data framework that allows for careful measuring and assessment.

The following list provides a top-level view of the SDGs. They are often presented in color-coded tables or wheels to facilitate conversation about their interlinked objectives. Every attempt has been made to make them clear, understandable, and assessable, and to connect them to earlier international agreements.

The United Nations Sustainable Development Goals

- Goal 1: No Poverty
- Goal 2: Zero Hunger
- Goal 3: Good Health and Well-being
- Goal 4: Quality Education
- Goal 5: Gender Equality
- Goal 6: Clean Water and Sanitation
- Goal 7: Affordable and Clean Energy
- Goal 8: Decent Work and Economic Growth
- Goal 9: Industry, Innovation and Infrastructure
- Goal 10: Reduced Inequality
- Goal 11: Sustainable Cities and Communities
- Goal 12: Responsible Consumption and Production
- Goal 13: Climate Action
- Goal 14: Life Below Water
- Goal 15: Life on Land
- Goal 16: Peace, Justice and Strong Institutions
- Goal 17: Partnerships for the Goals

A useful example is the first goal, SDG #1: No Poverty. This foundational objective makes a specific appeal to eradicate extreme poverty by reducing the proportion of people living below a nation's poverty line by at least half. The initiative proposes to do this by increasing access to decent wages, health insurance, retirement programs, and other social services, as well as providing basic necessities like drinking water and electricity. SDG #1 also asks governments and organizations to prepare for and address the negative economic impact of natural disasters and other emergencies, which drive people into poverty.

Readers may wonder if this goal is primarily for global audiences, or if it relates in tangible ways to the United States. The answer may be surprising. Near the end of 2019, over 39 million people lived below the poverty line in the U.S., defined as individuals who earned less than $35 per day. This figure included nearly 11 million children, or approximately 1 in 7 young people in the United States. Poverty is a major problem in the U.S. because there is a growing gap between rich and poor. It means that millions of people lack access to housing, education, health services, clean water, and basic sanitation.

SDG #1: No Poverty raises awareness about this problem in every country, so that governments and social impact organizations can develop solutions to the challenge. In the U.S., thousands of agencies are focusing on the most pressing issues, but the need is still very great.

As we noted at the beginning of the chapter, we can't address the world's social and environmental challenges unless we acknowledge the actual problems we're facing. The UN SDGs help with this work by directing our attention to common problems that exist around the world. The UN has collected millions of data points from over 200 countries, gathered from national data sources that were compiled by international agencies.

Covid-19 and the SDGs

The 17 UN SDGs had only been active for a few years when the Covid-19 pandemic arrived in late 2019. By the end of 2022, the United Nations estimated that Covid-19 had erased four years of gains against poverty worldwide, because the pandemic produced illness, hardship, and death in communities around the world that were severely disrupted. The number of people in poverty globally rose from 581 million in 2020 to approximately 660 million in 2022. The money promised to help these communities by government organizations was also in short supply. In many cases, the Covid-19 funding designed to support local communities never arrived.[8]

Although working to mitigate global poverty seems daunting, it is inspiring to see how many innovators are at work addressing this issue. For example, in the U.S. there were over 64,500 nonprofit organizations addressing SDG #1 in 2022. The average annual income received by each of these organization was $3 million, and the total revenues received in the poverty-support sector was $212 billion. For each of the UN SDGs it is a similar story. There are literally thousands of social impact organizations at work addressing a range of human and environmental challenges. What the $2.8 trillion sector needed most, however, was a mechanism to track progress toward the goals and highlight the critical opportunities that exist in the sector.

Tools for Measuring Success

In 2017, Shelly Cano Kurtz and Luis Salazar founded a social impact incubator called Giving Tech Labs to help social entrepreneurs use emerging technology to address pressing challenges. They had helped dozens of social impact organizations with content strategy and go-to-market planning. However, they soon realized there were *thousands* of social innovators who wanted the industry data and insights that they were collecting.

Digital transformation had become a must-have for nonprofit organizations, and the social impact sector was in the midst of a gradual transformation from traditional business methods to digital-first offerings. Although many firms were using the UN SDGs to target their activities, it was unclear *where* the opportunities were and *who* might be a good partner.

Social entrepreneurs and funders were "flying blind" as they tried to deploy resources and personnel to start new projects. Without a directory of products and services, tech for good startups were inadvertently reinventing the wheel as they designed solutions that another organization had already brought to market. In addition, data about outcomes and revenue in the sector was incomplete and hard to access. There was no easy way to spot "service deserts"— that is, areas where there were few, if any, solutions that addressed the UN Sustainable Development Goals. It was also impossible to survey the evolving social impact marketplace in real time.

In 2018, Shelly and Luis hired a chief scientist, Dr. Ying Li, to help them create a data mining and analysis strategy around a large dataset they had assembled about active social impact projects. Using Internal Revenue Service (IRS) reports and corporate disclosure statements, the team collected information about a range of for-profit and nonprofit firms that were committed to socially beneficial causes. Dr. Li built a massive data aggregator and advisory services tool that could generate deep insights about social impact work, organizing the results in different market *domains* (or areas). The team had an ambitious goal. They wanted to identify trusted sources of information, extract and display essential data, discover symbiotic relationships among companies, and derive social innovation insights that could help emerging organizations with decision making.

Rather than just *reporting* the information, however, they wanted to spur the creation of *new social enterprises*. In other words, Giving Tech Labs wanted to build a startup incubator where thousands of new startups could interact and share information to address social and environmental problems. When the team presented their ideas at the 2019 Amazon Web Services Imagine Nonprofit Conference, representatives of dozens of funders and social impact organizations wanted to hear more.

The data analysis tool and website they demonstrated became known as X4i.org (now Giving Compass Insights). The initial prototype was supported by additional investments from the Ford Foundation, Hewlett Foundation, Rockefeller Foundation, Microsoft Corporation, and others. In 2020, X4i.org was launched as a for-profit business (https://x4i.org) with a mission to support the rapid expansion of the social impact sector. In particular, X4i.org was designed to support tech for good organizations to address local and global needs. X4i.org became Giving Compass Insights in late 2023, after being acquired by Giving Compass Network. The marketplace has strongly supported this information source and social innovation model.

X4i.org offers a unique collection of industry reports, custom datasets, and sector briefs that any person can use to understand how the social impact sector works. Using a simple point-and-click user interface, a researcher can determine which UN SDGs are being addressed by a solution and where new opportunities lie. The team behind X4i.org uses data mining and analysis algorithms to aggregate, classify, and organize over 800 million units of knowledge gathered from public filings and IRS reports. Some of the information is free to access at X4i.org, and custom reports are also available for a fee.

Figure 2.1 shows the Giving Compass Insights website in late 2023, with its colorful graphical wheel and attractive user interface. UN SDG #1: No Poverty is the impact category selected for this image. At the time of the book's publication, there were 130 tech solutions related to SDG #1 in the tech directory. The annual funding for this sector in the U.S. was $212 billion in 2022. A product summary for each tech solution is available, along with links to the solution, badges, industry awards, and additional information. Using a few clicks, it is now possible to examine thousands of social impact companies and view their specific offerings.

The availability of the X4i.org website and data aggregation tool is an important development for social innovators. It allows new and experienced practitioners to explore existing solutions and find organizations to partner with. It is also a viable job search tool, providing contact information for thousands of social impact companies. We'll return to the Giving Compass Insights tech directory regularly in the book. To learn a bit more about Giving Compass Insights now, open a web browser and visit https://x4i.org.

Identifying Needs in the Community

The overall marketplace for social impact work in the U.S. is $2.8 trillion, which is twice as big as the commercial banking industry in the U.S., and 28 times larger than the entire U.S. video game industry. However, it is helpful to set aside the financial implications of this for a moment and consider the information as an insight into *unmet needs in the community*, where people urgently need services and support. Using the Giving Compass Insights tool, it is easy to see how the different subfields measure up.

For example, Table 2.1 shows the total revenue received for six UN SDG funding categories. (For the moment, we are focusing on

Figure 2.1 The Giving Compass Insights website (X4i.org) with tech solutions related to UN SDG #1: No Poverty selected.

Table 2.1 Total revenue received for six UN SDG funding categories

UN Sustainable Development Goal	U.S. Revenues in 2022
1. Good Health and Well-being (SDG #3)	$1.6 trillion
2. Quality Education (SDG #4)	$428 billion
3. Decent Work and Economic Growth (SDG #8)	$350 billion
4. No Poverty (SDG #1)	$212 billion
5. Sustainable Cities (SDG #11)	$209 billion
6. Reduced Inequality (SDG #10)	$100 billion

the U.S. marketplace only.) The size of each investment category is large, because each row represents hundreds (or thousands) of organizations working in partnership across the United States.

Although just the first six SDGs are listed here, it is apparent how widely the categories vary in revenues. Predictably, healthcare is one of the most active sectors, coming in at $1.6 trillion in 2022. However, education ($428 billion) is also a location for major investment by government agencies, foundations, and private institutions. The tech directory also allows users to examine economic activity that is not specifically related to the UN SDGs, such as the amount of money spent on improving outcomes for marginalized groups, including seniors, women, LGBTQ+ groups, and disabled citizens. (This amount was $39.1 billion in 2022.)

Social Impact Innovation

The goal of this section has been to highlight many of the work opportunities that are available in the social impact sector, including recent initiatives in tech for good companies. There has never been a better time to learn social innovation principles.

Social impact innovation emerged in the U.S. during a period of rapid technological innovation, when new infrastructures in transportation, communication, housing, and healthcare raised life expectancy and living standards across the country. However, not everyone benefited equally from these innovations, and it was often left to community organizations to distribute resources equitably and support neglected populations. We now use the comprehensive term "social impact organization" to describe the work that these groups do to address social, environmental, and economic issues. Social impact innovators can be for-profit corporations, nonprofit organizations, government entities, or educational institutions. The Giving Compass Insights tech directory allows new and experienced practitioners to study business activity in this sector and spot new business opportunities.

The remainder of this book focuses on the skills and mindsets needed by social impact practitioners, especially leaders who direct and inspire tech for good teams. We'll present social innovation techniques that will help you transform empathy into action, and use emerging technologies to create socially beneficial solutions at scale. We begin with an exploration of digital transformation strategies, and a case study that shows how low-cost, scalable technologies were used to protect child abuse survivors and victims of crime.

Notes

1 United Nations, *The Sustainable Development Goals Report 2022* (New York: United Nations Publications, 2022), 2.
2 Robert J. Gordon, *The Rise and Fall of American Growth* (Princeton: Princeton University Press, 2016), 4.
3 Carl Benedikt Frey, *The Technology Trap: Capital, Labor, and Power in the Age of Automation* (Princeton: Princeton University Press, 2019), 155.
4 Important discussions of inequity in the U.S. during the "technology surge" of the early twentieth century include Richard Rothstein, *The Color of Law: A Forgotten History of How Our Government Segregated America* (New York: W.W. Norton, 2018); and Beth Tompkins Bates, *The Making of Black Detroit in the Age of Henry Ford* (Chapel Hill: The University of North Carolina Press, 2012).
5 X4Impact, "State of the Market for Social Innovators" (June 2022), 3.
6 X4Impact, "State of the Market for Social Innovators" (June 2022), 6.
7 UN Resolution A/RES/70/1, "Transforming our World: The 2030 Agenda for Sustainable Development" (October 2015), 1.
8 United Nations, *The Sustainable Development Goals Report* (2022), 10.

3 Digital Transformation Strategies

In the twentieth century, technological innovation laid the groundwork for numerous social and environmental initiatives around the world. In the business sector, one of the most consequential shifts has been the change from mechanical and analogue technologies to the use of digital systems for record keeping, communication, manufacturing, and delivering services. Since the 2010s, the rapid integration of digital technology into all areas of an organization's workflow has been referred to as *digital transformation*.

Digital transformation implies the integration of digital technology into all areas of a business operation to streamline operations and add value. The results include increased accuracy, faster delivery, cost savings, and waste reduction. When applied to social impact firms, digital transformation is an organizational *indicator* to potential partners and the community. It signifies that there has been a fundamental change in how a firm delivers products and services to its clients. The term is aspirational and implies operational efficiency, readiness for purpose-driven work, and challenging the status quo.

This chapter introduces digital transformation as a pathway to achieving social and environmental outcomes in tech for good companies. We explore how digital transformation can set the stage for meaningful contributions to a range of projects and initiatives, including benchmarks set out by the United Nations Sustainable Development Goals (UN SDGs). We also discuss useful skills and mindsets for employees managing institutional change.

Our featured case study presents Guardify, an award-wining tech for good company in Nebraska that protects child abuse survivors and victims of crime. Like Forestmatic, Guardify uses tech for good principles to meet community needs by leveraging low-cost, scalable technologies. We'll examine Guardify's digital transformation strategy and then identify key components of digitization that can be applied to any social impact organization.

If you're new to social impact work, this chapter will help you understand how organizations are using scalable technology for the

DOI: 10.4324/9781003465669-3

public good. Many of the solutions are simple and cost-effective, including "gig economy" tools and proven techniques that come from the general market. Ultimately, digital transformation can be as simple as using existing systems and networks more effectively to help organizations reduce costs and create optimized workflows. By harnessing the power of a shared system, you can gain valuable information that is not readily available when systems are decentralized.

Innovating to Protect Children and Enable Justice

The social challenge that Guardify first addressed begins with a sobering fact: Over 700,000 children per year are abused in the United States. When a traumatic event is reported, children and families get support from prosecutors, law enforcement agencies, trauma specialists, and a child advocacy center. There are currently about 1,000 independent nonprofits related to this work sprinkled throughout the country in urban and rural areas, each accredited by the National Children's Alliance based in Washington, DC.

A child forensic interview is usually one of the first steps in investigating child abuse and preserving important details. The interview is typically recorded on video, to prevent the child from having to share their deepest secrets multiple times, recounting their most violating moments, helping to reduce the potential for post-traumatic stress disorder (PTSD).

When there is an allegation of abuse, a trained child interviewer conducts a forensic interview to document the child's experiences in an age-appropriate manner. The child forensic interview is the heart of the case, often considered the most valuable piece of evidence. A designated agency of record is responsible to safeguard the interview and provide access to other officials upon request. For decades, this process was manual. Law enforcement agencies and child protection experts from multiple jurisdictions worked together as part of a multidisciplinary team. That could mean up to ten copies of a single video recording would be required. Video recordings needed to be duplicated or "burned" onto a physical tape, DVD, USB, or hard drive to provide access to each of the organizations working on the case. The process is documented through a complex chain of custody. Before digital transformation, the agencies involved might use a "sign out sheet" with paper logs in binders or filing cabinets, and the original video might get stored under lock and key.

Securing and managing highly sensitive video recordings became more and more of a challenge as new video formats allowed for increased video capture and distribution. There were different formats to manage, and the danger of inadvertently releasing recordings or images became a great concern. Often, officials locked up video testimonies in filing cabinets or stored them off-site in storage units, where they became extremely difficult to work with. In some cases, boxes of VHS tapes and DVDs piled up with no long-term strategy for preservation or access. As a result, it could take weeks to track down forensic recordings. In some cases, the fragile media had already deteriorated.

Even for new cases, agency partners were challenged to access interviews in a timely manner. Often, investigators would drive for hours to watch or retrieve video evidence. Videos were also sent via physical mailing—taking days to arrive. Annotations, transcripts, and closed captioning systems were also manual or hybrid processes.

The red tape involved with storing and transporting video recordings cost taxpayers millions of dollars each year with no clear benefit. In many cases, trained forensic interviewers, including clinical child psychologists and social workers, spent as much time on administrative video support work (burning and routing videos) as documenting child victim statements.

In 2018, Giving Tech Labs went to Omaha, Nebraska, to listen and learn from nonprofit practitioners and philanthropic funders about priority challenges and how they might be solved through social innovation. Sara Boyd was the CEO of the Omaha Community Foundation, and she agreed to host listening sessions to learn how to accelerate positive outcomes through technology. During the focus group, a leader from Project Harmony raised his hand to ask for help.

Project Harmony is one of the leading child advocacy centers in the U.S., conducting over 6,000 child forensic interviews each year and providing training sessions to the broader field of child protection and investigative agencies. Even as an industry leader, they lacked modern processes to easily secure and manage multimedia files.

Finding a way to streamline the forensic interview process was a reoccurring problem. In a case Project Harmony described, a zealous defense attorney made unauthorized copies of a child's video interview and distributed them to the defendant's family. The judge had to throw out the case because of mishandling of evidence. From that day on, the group was committed to preventing this from happening to other children.

The organizations also lacked a backup system to protect video recordings from loss or damage. When evidence did disappear, a child would have to retell and relive their trauma. Numerous agencies also needed access to this sensitive material. This could include law enforcement agencies, child advocacy peers, child protective services, the local district attorney's office, the defense attorney, and sometimes more.

At the meeting in Omaha, the Project Harmony speaker explained that the process was cumbersome because it involved routing and preserving *outdated technology*. The entire process seemed like a good candidate for *digital transformation*, or a change in how the agencies interacted with each other and managed materials. For starters, a digital solution could help them with the task of managing video recordings, which would help protect children in Nebraska and elsewhere.

Deploying a Cloud-Based Solution

When Giving Tech Labs considered the problem, they listened carefully to the needs of stakeholders, conducted cursory market research, and then recommended a cloud-based digital storage solution that would be secure and user-friendly for all officials who needed access to forensic interviews. Importantly, it could also prevent access to unauthorized individuals.

Instead of recommending a "work for hire" scenario, building a solution that only benefited Omaha, Shelly Cano Kurtz and her team formed a small startup *incubation* to develop core video management technologies that could also be used elsewhere. One of their goals was to build a point-and-click user interface that would be easy to control for non-technical users. If successful, Shelly and her team knew the solution could be scaled to serve thousands of organizations across the country.

In other words, the digital transformation process for one nonprofit agency (Project Harmony) would allow for the development of a solution that could be an industry standard to protect all digital evidence, using the software-as-a-service (SaaS) revenue model.

After initial success and a financing round, the story came full circle. Sara Boyd, the enterprising CEO of the Omaha Community Foundation, became the first CEO of the new startup. The company was called VidaNyx. As a private corporation, VidaNyx was purpose-built to center its work, as Guardify does today, on the "justice" attribute of UN SDG #16: Peace, Justice, and Strong Institutions. The aim of this goal is to promote peaceful and inclusive societies, ensure access to justice for all, and build effective, accountable institutions at all levels.

The organization's purpose was rooted in empathy and compassion, which led them to critique existing procedures and think about how their actions could support children and families. SDG #16 is also concerned with impact initiatives that address criminal justice, along with voting rights, foster care, and government transparency.

Less than nine months after that first meeting in Omaha, a tech for good company was built with a mission to enable justice and healing. The for-profit software business now operates under the name Guardify, as a cloud-based digital evidence management company. Guardify also works to *accelerate* the pace of justice and healing for survivors of serious crime. The system protects forensic interviews but also securely routes them to authorized team members, vastly improving the speed at which evidence is reviewed. When child advocacy centers use Guardify, they no longer need to make copies of forensic interviews on VHS tape, DVDs, or Zip drive media. They can simply upload a digital recording to the secure web portal, and each agency or advocate will have immediate access to the secure data with built-in features to support collaboration and investigation. The system is designed to optimize the entire "journey" that recorded testimony makes, from recording to routing, review, storage, and archiving—all with a complete digital chain of custody.

Five years after its founding, Guardify is a highly successful tech for good company. In mid-2023, tech sector veteran Ben Jackson replaced Sara Boyd as CEO, bringing cross-functional industry experience and a wealth of knowledge about emerging technology. The organization is still run by a small group of dedicated changemakers with less than 20 full-time employees. Next to the CEO, there are software engineers (focusing on digitizing and optimizing a variety of media files, cloud computing, and web development), a product designer, a marketing manager, a finance leader, a small sales team, and employees that manage customer success. In outreach roles, Guardify has decades of subject-matter expertise in the fields of child abuse investigations and prosecution.

This rich cross-sector experience is valuable for the young enterprise—not just to grow, but to grow intentionally based on real-time feedback from those with lived experience. When an organization is promoting emerging digital solutions to nonprofits and government agencies, conveying credibility and creating customer intimacy is paramount.

Using Success Metrics

Digital transformation enables a range of success metrics that an organization can report to its partners. To show that they have reduced the *total cost of ownership*, Guardify tracks and reports data about the cost savings related to evidence management, time savings for agencies, and other metrics to provide insights from the aggregate data. For example, they save the average age of interview subjects, the average length of interviews, regional distinctions, and more. By the end of 2023, Guardify reported 213,000 forensic videos protected, uploaded via their secure web portal. This evidence was handled over 10.2 million times by trusted partners in law enforcement and other authorized agencies. The company reports a savings of up to 90 percent of the total cost per case, when comparing Guardify to the traditional method of video routing and storage.

By late 2023, over 53,000 users have accessed forensic video evidence digitally through Guardify, allowing them to do their job better. More than 12,500 agencies across the U.S. trust Guardify to access digital evidence. The top four agency types using the product are law enforcement (45%), child protective services (25%), prosecution (11%), and child advocacy centers (8%). Law enforcement officers alone saved over 145,000 hours procuring and tracking video evidence.

How does Guardify generate revenue to support its stakeholders? Guardify's digital transformation strategy has been to organize itself as an SaaS enterprise. This type of company delivers software products for a subscription fee over the web, offering its features "on demand" for customers. Rather than installing data and tools on a user's hard disk, an SaaS company manages software and data for the customer remotely "in the cloud" (or via distributed servers on the Internet). This is an ideal business model for Guardify, because the company can securely manage access to video recordings and images via military-grade encryption technology, watermarking, and two-factor authentication.

Guardify received early funding from organizations that believe in its social mission to protect children and other victims of crime. With help from Giving Tech Labs, Guardify hired software engineers and designers to re-orient the traditional approach to recording and distributing evidence. They focused on the customer experience, reducing friction in the routing of evidence, increasing speed, creating *digital literacy*, and elevating impact through scale. To increase its revenue and impact, Guardify refined their subscription model and differentiated their product line using different tiers and offerings, based on customer needs. Ultimately, their success is tied to getting nonprofits and government agencies to recognize the value and cost savings in their product. As more and more customers adopt the product, it will become a sustainable industry standard to help modernize the U.S. court system and victim advocacy.

Beyond financial and technical measures, Guardify is inspiring because they focus their business on purpose-driven goals and objectives. Their work aligns with accelerating justice and enabling healing, values that are represented by SDG #16 and SDG #3. The team created a scalable solution that offers value to law enforcement, child advocacy, and the justice system but also shows potential for profit and growth. For all of these reasons, Guardify (VidaNyx) was recognized as one of Nebraska's top-ranked tech startups in 2021 and 2022.

Digital Transformation Frameworks

Digital transformation involves the integration of digital technology into all areas of an organization's workflow, including how a firm operates and how it delivers products and services to others. Organizations need to approach this task carefully, so that they can achieve a positive return on investment (ROI) from any capital that they invest in new technology or procedures.

Social impact organizations need to be particularly sensitive to ROI, because they may have shorter profitability horizons than traditional corporations.

Executives that lead organizations through the transformation process oversee a strategic planning cycle sometimes called *change management*. They typically meet with IT groups to consider the potential benefit of new technologies and plan how they will be evaluated, budgeted for, and deployed. Many organizations purchase enterprise resource planning (ERP) software such as Microsoft Dynamics 365 to replace their manual procedures with digital-first processes that are carefully integrated. An ERP system can manage regular business activities in a comprehensive way by using a common user interface and data model. These integrated activities typically include accounting, procurement, project management, human resources, and supply chain operations.

In whatever way a social impact organization achieves it, the goal of digital transformation is to *maximize the social good that the company achieves while focusing on efficiency and eliminating unnecessary expenditures.*

Ideally, digitalization will support this process, because new technology can often streamline existing processes and amplify the work that social impact firms do.[1] However, technology for its own sake is not the goal. Positively impacting customers and communities is.

For example, imagine that you decide to open a small clothing store near a local hospital to provide comfortable, handmade goods to patients that have just received medical care. As you prepare for opening day, you remember that you need a point-of-sale system to receive revenue, record purchases, and issue receipts. Would you build your own point-of-sale system and write the software to run it? Or would you purchase an existing point-of-sale system to handle your transactions?

The answer to this question seems obvious: You would shop around and buy an existing point-of-sale system, because you are not in the cash register business, you are in the handmade goods business, with a heart for those who are recovering from challenging medical procedures. Social impact organizations should follow similar logic as they approach digital transformation opportunities. They should focus on the social cause that they understand and know well, and buy or lease the digital solutions that will help them manage business tasks.

The Guardify company used similar logic when they approached the digital aspects of their business. The value of Guardify's digital offerings arose from the ability to provide peace of mind and easy access to sensitive material that was formerly stored on tapes and locked in cabinets. Digital transformation supported this core business function, but the team's business systems and communication strategies were often built around existing digital technologies.

A Digital Transformation Checklist

During its planning process, the Guardify team needed to evaluate whether the problems they were hoping to solve could be addressed by a new digital solution or if an existing tool was available. This discernment process was vital for their organization to complete, and how they approached the process changed their entire outlook.

The checklist they used is a helpful resource for most social impact organizations to consider. We present it here as a helpful self-assessment tool for all organizations that are considering digital transformation:

1. **Is it useful or necessary to digitalize a common task?** This foundational question recognizes that some procedures in an organization are ripe for improvement, while others are fine as they are. If there isn't a clear benefit to using digital technology, consider leaving the process as it is. (If your answer is "no" here, you don't need a new technology or system.)
2. **Is this the right process to transform?** If you have a candidate for digital transformation, be sure to carefully *map out* the

problem before you design something new around it. In the rush to find digital-first solutions, some companies embed inefficiencies into their new procedures. Sort out the details first.

3. **Is the problem unique to your organization?** An ideal candidate for digital transformation is a task or problem that many organizations *share*. (If you answer "yes" here, your solution may be so unique to your firm that it cannot be applied to others.) However, with some creative thinking, you may be able to find some aspect of your solution that relates to the situation of others.

4. **Is a solution already available?** If you share problems with other organizations, it may be that a partner or technology vendor has already created a technical fix for your problem. Do some research, and if you find something that can be used or adapted, license it rather than creating a "one-off" solution.

5. **Is this a shared "pain point"?** In some cases, you'll find that other organizations *do* have the same problem, and no ready-made solutions are available. In this case, there might be enough common ground to build a new scalable innovation that can be sold to others. Although a shared pain point sounds negative, it also represents an *opportunity for innovation*.

6. **Can you finance a new innovation?** Building a digital-first solution involves costs and business risk. Can you find a way to finance your solution so that others can share the financial burden? For example, could you develop a digital solution and sell it on the web to those who need it? (Perhaps via an SaaS model?) To maximize your return on investment, it's appropriate to get those who will benefit from the solution to help pay for it.

7. **Will customers share data and information?** If your solution relies on information, consider carefully where you will get the data, and whether your customers will freely share it with you. This is largely a psychological question. In the Technology for the Public Interest sector, many tech for good companies ask partners to share or distribute portions of their business data freely, while protecting the sensitive information that needs to remain private. (For more information about data choices, see Chapter 7.)

As this self-assessment indicates, deciding whether to build a new digital solution or not requires careful discernment. In some cases, there is a large potential market for solutions that match widespread needs. But in other situations, there are few partners who will benefit from a collaborative solution. Importantly, if there is already a technology fix in the marketplace, it is important to understand what the solution offers and if it can be reused, even in part, to meet your needs. Duplicating the effort of others is rarely a good idea. But there are many creative ways to use existing systems and infrastructures.

The Pace of Digitalization

Digital transformation practices vary widely, and the way that individual organizations approach the process will be different for each company. The overall pace of digitalization depends on an organization's size, its management structures, and the sector in which it operates.

Most mature social impact organizations will have a mixture of work habits and offerings that are digital in nature. Recent surveys show that organizations with physical goods to warehouse and distribute are usually slower to digitally enhance their procedures. By contrast, the pace of digitization has been faster in the healthcare, pharma, and financial sectors, where corporate leaders have found it easier to embrace digital-first offerings, especially since the Covid-19 pandemic.[2]

Think of digital transformation as a continuum. Some organizations are just *beginning* to experiment with new digital processes and technologies. A typical scenario for newcomers is that digital-first experiments are taking place in isolated groups around the company. Each new digital enhancement or solution shows potential, but digital experiments are not widely coordinated, and executives are not yet convinced of their value. Many workers still rely on legacy systems that require significant costs and maintenance.

Organizations that are farther along the digitization pathway have a *unified strategy* for digital-first products and procedures. These firms have recognized that adopting new technologies is essential, and they often have goals for achieving positive ROI for expenditures related to technology. Executives may speak about their commitment to digital transformation. They may even reward innovation best practices and hire new talent to break down barriers. However, the inertia related to manual procedures and legacy systems continues to influence how the company operates. Structurally, the company shows progress towards digital transformation, but the benefits are not fully realized. Numerous "silos" remain around the company that are resistant to change.

Organizations that emerge as true *digital-first companies* are thoroughly renovated by the digital transformation process. They are led by changemakers who have clearly articulated a vision for enterprise-wide innovation. They tend to work faster, are connected more fully to clients and customers, and have a unified message about digital-first and digital enhancement. They innovate rapidly, learning from each success and failure. In many tech for good companies, this process is guided by so-called "Agile" methods, a term originating from the iterative software development procedures that emerged in the 1990s and 2000s. Agile methods stress the rapid "bootstrapping" of projects, continuous improvement, and regular feedback from clients and customers.[3] Agile companies also measure and track data so that it can be used to respond to changing conditions and speed up business procedures.

Digital transformation is often easier for an organization that is new or *organized around digital-first principles*. This is why tech for good firms are so fascinating to study, because embedding scalable technology in their organization is usually part of their core orientation to the market. However, digital transformation doesn't always mean a company is using the most recent or the most expensive technology. It simply means that traditional ways of doing business have been replaced by streamlined systems and procedures. This includes how groups function internally and handle traditional business tasks like interacting with clients, gathering data, communicating internally, managing the supply chain, reporting to stakeholders, and so on.

Digital transformation is essentially a mindset that asks organizations to continually reflect on the following questions:

- How can we improve the way that we are doing things?
- How can we adapt to new opportunities and threats?
- How can emerging technical systems help us do this work?

Before social impact organizations take on new purpose-driven projects, we recommend that they evaluate their readiness for digital transformation. Digital-first readiness is important not only for the product they produce, but for the internal procedures within the organization. We recommend the following readiness indicators for organizations that are evaluating their procedures.

Digital-First Readiness: Is Your Organization Ready to Innovate?

- How can your purpose-driven project be enhanced or scaled by digitization?
- Are there common tasks in your business or sector that can be improved or scaled?

- Is there a part of the customer or client experience that could be improved?
- Can communication within your organization be enhanced by new systems or procedures?
- Do the groups in your organization use different tools to communicate with clients and employees? Is there a clear reason why you are using different or incompatible systems?
- Can internal business operations be more sustainable or resilient if unified technologies or procedures are used? Should your company consider an integrated ERP system?
- Is data in your organization stored in one integrated system? Is it widely available to all employees?
- Are employees able to make predictions using data? Can they optimize processes as conditions change?
- How are goods or raw materials moved within your organization? Does your firm have a supply chain that could be optimized by digitalization?
- Would productivity or company culture be improved by working or meeting remotely? Have you adopted a unified communication platform, such as Microsoft Teams or Zoom?
- Might cloud-based solutions help your organization to share, distribute, or safeguard information?
- How might sensitive data be managed and secured in your organization?
- Are there low-cost tools available in your firm that you can use in new ways (such as Microsoft 365 or Google Workplace)?
- Can you distribute information more effectively via a website, social media, or mobile applications?
- Can AI-enhanced tools help you create value for customers or streamline procedures?
- Can you make improvements to employee training or corporate on-boarding with new technology?
- Can ethics or corporate governance be improved by using a digital-first solution?

Low-Cost Tools and Infrastructure

A list of digital-readiness indicators is valuable, but it can also be somewhat abstract. Is digital transformation really about buying new products? Or is it related to applying efficient management principles to an organization? At the outset, we want to clarify that optimizing your procedures is *not* only about deploying new software systems. Digital-first also means *using existing systems and networks more effectively* to help your organization reduce costs and provide innovative solutions. Often, this involves thinking creatively about low-cost tools and infrastructures that already exist.

Consider the following list of global infrastructures that have been developed over the past decade. How can your organization leverage these systems without incurring the cost of creating them? In late 2023, our planet had:

- 6.8 billion smartphones
- 4.9 billion daily Internet users
- 3 billion users of Google Workspace apps
- 2.9 billion monthly Facebook users
- 1.4 billion users of Microsoft Windows 10 or 11
- 1 billion monthly TikTok users
- 505 million monthly podcast listeners
- 345 million users of Microsoft 365
- 141 million active players of Minecraft (monthly)

Consider how expensive these infrastructures were to create, but how inexpensive it is for people to use them to develop or distribute digital solutions. Systems like this allow you to lower the cost of a solution, reduce constraints, and increase your competitiveness. For example, if you deploy a mobile application using the Apple Store, it can be downloaded by millions of iPhone, iPad, and Apple Watch users. You incur the costs of creating and supporting the mobile application, but you don't develop the smartphone infrastructure.

The nonprofit organization Code.org followed this logic when it adopted the Minecraft platform to teach young people how to take their first steps with computer programming. Code.org realized that millions of young people were playing Minecraft, so they created modules that adapted the game so that it could be used to teach fundamental coding concepts. Code.org partnered with Microsoft (the owner of Minecraft), rather than creating a competitive platform with no installed base. This worked well because both organizations want to increase the number of young people learning to code. As a creative social impact organization, Code.org used an existing, low-cost infrastructure with impressive results.[4]

While the list we shared emphasizes commercial digital infrastructures, there are many free or low-cost systems that can be combined creatively by social impact organizations, including technologies that were deployed years ago. Preparing for digital transformation means considering all the ways that an organization can increase its efficiency, including methods that are no longer breaking news.

For example, consider the low-cost systems used by "gig economy" workers over the last decade, a labor market characterized by part-time projects and freelance work. Gig economy employees often act as independent contractors, using a combination of smartphones, laptops, and low-cost productivity tools to complete their tasks. They tend to use hybrid or public work spaces, cloud-based solutions, social media, AI, and free Wi-Fi—leveraging public infrastructures whenever possible.

Social impact organizations should take note of these strategies, which demonstrate the effective use of low-cost infrastructures in our economy. In organizations that have access to pre-installed productivity tools, consider the benefit of using Google Workplace, Microsoft 365, or ChatGPT to manage inventories, track customers, or handle electronic communication. This approach is a cost-effective path to digital transformation, and much more practical than building a custom solution with expensive design, implementation, and maintenance.

There is an important sustainability message to emphasize here: Organizations should "eat their own dog food" when it comes to efficiency, meaning that before they advocate for sustainable practices, they should be as sustainable as possible with their own business procedures. Another way of expressing this principle is "practice what you preach."

Finally, as firms approach the digital transformation continuum, they should consider *all* the infrastructures that exist in local and regional communities as they plan. Leveraging both digital and physical infrastructures will help organizations reduce costs and remain nimble. Physical infrastructures include electrical grids, lighting, radio, water and waste systems, public transit, roads, automobiles, airplanes, boats, ports, and airwaves. Additional social structures include government organizations, healthcare systems, education networks (public and private), religious organizations, ride sharing systems, worker training programs, research institutions, libraries, business clubs, charitable foundations, hiking trails, and more.

Digital transformation is ultimately concerned with enhancing operational agility, improving the customer experience, and making an organization more sustainable over the long term. In many cases, this can be achieved by evaluating the systems that are available and leveraging existing networks. If a product already exists in the marketplace, don't reinvent the wheel. Buy or license what you find, share what you have, and partner creatively with others.

Pathways to Social Impact

The goal of this chapter has been to present digital transformation as a measure of innovation readiness and a pathway to social impact. If you are new to the social impact sector, this mindset will be helpful to you as you prepare for a range of jobs and innovation opportunities.

The Guardify company used digital transformation to protect children and reduce the expense of preserving and distributing forensic evidence. They created digital tools and methods to help child advocacy employees be more productive in their daily work. At first, they used cloud computing and encryption software to safeguard sensitive data. But over time they used a range of digital tools to help their employees collaborate with others and make business decisions.

Guardify also harnessed the UN SDG framework to communicate their social mission. They continually focused on value creation in the marketplace by asking three questions: "How can we improve the way that we are doing things?" "How can technical systems help us do this work?" "How can we scale solutions so that others can benefit from them?"

In the next chapter, we focus on the "Why?" of social innovation projects. We discuss creative ways to embed purpose into social impact organizations, and how to ground projects in community values such as equity, compassion, and person-to-person engagement. We'll present several case studies that demonstrate this approach, including creative social impact organizations that support people living with physical, mental, and sensory impairment. Embedding purpose into projects is a commitment that clarifies goals and benefits both community members and employees.

Notes

1 For a useful discussion of the amplifying role of technology, and its limitations, see Kentaro Toyama, *Geek Heresy: Rescuing Social Change from the Cult of Technology* (New York: PublicAffairs, 2015), esp. Chapter 2: "The Law of Amplification."
2 A helpful report to study the pace of digital transformation in companies is McKinsey & Company, "How COVID-19 has pushed companies over the technology tipping point—and transformed business forever" (2020). www.mckinsey.com/capabilities/strategy-and-corporate-finance/our-insights/how-covid-19-has-pushed-companies-over-the-

technology-tipping-point-and-transformed-business-forever. Accessed December 5, 2023.
3 Three popular Agile methods are Scrum, Kanban, and lean development. To see how this type of thinking can influence a social impact organization, see Ann Mei Chang, *Lean Impact: How to Innovate for Radically Greater Social Good* (New York: John Wiley & Sons, 2019).
4 The diffusion of technical skills like computational thinking and programming is an important aspect of digital transformation across the United States. Michael recently wrote a book about this process that features the experiences of students, scientists, educators, and social entrepreneurs. See Michael J. Halvorson, *Code Nation: Personal Computing and the Learn to Program Movement in America* (New York: ACM Books, 2020).

4 Embedding Purpose into Projects

Have you visited the website of a social impact organization recently?

Purpose-driven companies have much more to do than sell products and services via their online platforms. To be successful, they also need to highlight what they do, whom they serve, and why they complete their work. An important part of this presentation is usually the company's *mission statement*, which communicates the organization's core values and underlying purpose for operating.

A mission statement can be a very powerful tool for a social impact organization. When it summarizes the challenge an organization plans to address, it can serve as a guide to decision making and employee behavior. Successful companies often use mission statements to set priorities, align objectives, and inspire action.

For example, the United Way's mission statement indicates that the organization seeks to "improve lives by mobilizing the caring power of communities around the world to advance the common good."[1] The key term here is "mobilizing." The United Way hopes to bring people and resources together to build strong, equitable communities where everyone can thrive.

Although technology can be one of the tools that an organization uses to accomplish its mission, a mission statement rarely uses technical language to articulate its goals. Instead, a typical statement describes values, people, and social benefits in tangible ways. For example, a firm that focuses on United Nations Sustainable Development Goal #2: Zero Hunger might identify the *who* that is supported by their initiatives and a *why* that inspires action. A mission statement of this type might read: *We aspire to improve nutrition for children because we believe that having enough to eat is a basic human right.*

When an organization is unified around mission and purpose, it's often easier to accomplish goals and objectives. This is why there is so much talk in management circles about "purpose-driven organizations." Research shows that purpose-driven companies have higher productivity and growth rates than other firms, along

DOI: 10.4324/9781003465669-4

with more satisfied employees who tend to stay longer.[2] At the core of purpose-driven work is the recognition that each of us has something to do to support the communities we live in. This awareness is often personal and direct, drawing on an individual's sense of duty or vocation. Do you feel called to do work that contributes to the greater good of society? How can you creatively work with others for the good of others?

Companies thrive when they have leaders that model core values and connect purpose to organizational goals. In a recent industry report, McKinsey & Company found that the most important leadership traits to express in this regard are empathy and compassion. Leaders who emphasize these behaviors typically have three major strengths: They inspire others by building trust and common ground, they develop a broad vision for the future, and they lead by example.[3]

This chapter focuses on the "Why" that nourishes social innovation and inspires purpose-driven work in local and global contexts. We'll examine three leaders in the social impact sector who have shared a Why that inspires action and benefits vulnerable or marginalized groups. You'll learn about a social entrepreneur who started a tech company to assist people with speech disabilities and disorders; a foundation executive who funds systemic innovation related to communication disabilities; and a clothing designer who used *Shark Tank* to launch an adaptive clothing brand. Our goal is to inspire a new wave of social entrepreneurs who are purpose-driven and grounded in empathy, compassion, and community engagement.

Working to improve the lives of others is not just a task for do-gooders or idealists. Doing good for communities and our planet is a way to lead an extraordinary life, where you take your personal story, resources, and sense of vocation and share them with others to create powerful platforms for change.

The Right to Be Understood

Danny Weissberg is a gifted computer engineer and entrepreneur from Tel Aviv, Israel. Although Danny has a passion for tinkering with software, the idea for an important social innovation came to him when his family went through a healthcare crisis. How he responded to this challenge has benefited thousands of people around the world.[4]

In 2010, Danny's grandmother had a stroke. As a result, she lost the ability to speak in ways that could be understood by family members and caregivers. This medical crisis did not just impact

Danny's grandmother but the entire community. Once the center of her family network, the matriarch could no longer communicate with her friends or loved ones. Danny's relationship with his grandmother also deteriorated, as the disability impacted every aspect of her interaction with others. Speaking is a basic human need, but for Danny's grandmother, it was no longer possible in the way that she was accustomed to. In effect, she was trapped inside her body and unable to communicate with the outside world. Even the simplest daily tasks became a struggle.

Danny would never forget the sense of loss that came from her silencing.

What he came to understand, however, is that thousands of families are impacted by challenges related to irregular or non-standard speech. In fact, up to 100 million people in the world have a daily challenge in this area. It is an ongoing problem that has adverse effects on individuals as well as communities.

Non-standard speech is defined as speech that differs from the usual accepted, easily recognizable speech of native adult members of a particular speech community. Sometimes non-standard speech is the result of an injury or illness, such as a stroke. It may also be the result of a medical condition or a disability, such as ALS, cerebral palsy, Down syndrome, Parkinson's disease, throat cancer, or a muscular injury. Sometimes the normal aging process influences speech to a considerable extent. In addition, adults who are non-native speakers of a second or third language sometimes speak with an accent that is heavy enough that speech is challenging for community members to understand.

Irregular or non-standard speech is a *hidden disability* that impacts the quality of life for millions of individuals. As such, it is a neglected area of medical research and therapeutic care. A typical scenario is that a few family members or healthcare workers are able to interact with a non-standard speaker successfully, because they spend so much time with the disabled speaker, although the person is unintelligible to unfamiliar listeners. This leads to the need for "translation" between the non-standard speaker and community members. Although speech recognition tools such as Amazon's Alexa or Apple's Siri are helpful "hands-free" tools, they typically don't process non-standard speech, because they are designed to be used in so-called "typical" communication scenarios.

Empathy and Compassion

According to standard dictionaries, *empathy* is the capacity to step into another person's shoes, share their feelings, and understand one or more aspects of their life. Empathy is an essential emotion in human relationships, and it helps us build social connections with friends, neighbors, and the strangers that we meet. *Compassion* is a related term that implies both the sympathetic understanding of others *and action*. A person with compassion develops a feeling of concern for the unmet needs of another, coupled with a desire to alleviate that suffering.[5] Empathy and compassion are as important in the business world as they are in regular human life. Danny felt both emotions as he worked with his grandmother and interacted with communities impacted by speech-related disabilities.

Compassion involves physical changes in the human body and brain. It's a tactile experience. Our bodies communicate compassion through facial expressions, vocal signaling, and changes in posture. Compassion is also contemplative and action-oriented, playing a major role in world religions and spiritual traditions. Most of these systems are organized around the principle that if human beings can learn to be more compassionate, they will be more active in care for others and the self. If we cultivate compassion widely, many believe, the net effect will be the gradual improvement of human societies and the planet.

As Danny came to understand the suffering of people with non-standard speech, he discovered that millions of people around the world were challenged with this problem. His emotional response to the distress of his grandmother created an authentic desire to learn more and help. As part of the process, he reflected on his skills and interests, including his training as an engineer and his interest in tinkering with technology. Could there be a way to train a computer system to learn the sounds and word patterns of a person with non-standard speech? Danny believed the answer was "Yes!" The insight led him to a solution that would allow people to speak and be understood, no matter what their underlying medical condition, disability, disorder, or aging circumstance.

Danny reconnected with Stas Tiomkin, a gifted computer scientist completing doctoral work at the Hebrew University of Jerusalem. Stas was also a professor at the Technion Institute of Technology in Israel, where both men had completed their undergraduate studies. Danny remembered that Stas had an interest in speech recognition algorithms and the tools that engineers use to process digital audio. The two were also fascinated with Apple's iPhone and the iOS operating system, which had become important platforms for digital transformation in Israel, Europe, and the United States. They recognized the potential benefit of this expanding infrastructure, which provided millions of phone owners with an Internet connection, a microphone, a speaker, and an App Store to purchase software. Although less than 5 percent of the world's population experienced problems with non-standard speech, addressing this group could be a major opportunity to scale an important intervention. It could make a major difference in people's lives.

Danny and Stas took an interdisciplinary approach as they studied digital audio. They believed that language modeling, artificial intelligence, speech processing, and voice enhancement could all make major contributions to the problems they had encountered. Danny and Stas committed to starting a company that would test adaptive technologies and find ways to translate non-standard speech into something that would be more easily understood.

The group's first financial support came from a small development grant given by the government of Israel, followed by small "seed" contributions from a handful of investors. As the project gained momentum, the group became more expansive in their fundraising. The team entered several *social entrepreneurship contests* in Israel, Europe, and the United States. Each time that they received an award, they gained visibility and also had the opportunity to discuss their ideas with new mentors and contacts. The firm received several sustaining awards through this creative strategy, including a grant from the European Commission and a coveted innovation prize from the 43North Foundation of Buffalo, New York.

The team formally incorporated using the name Voiceitt. They began to understand their mission as supporting not only *individuals* with speech challenges but the entire *network* surrounding a person with non-standard speech. When Sara Smolley joined the organization as a third co-founder, she fine-tuned the organization's marketing to clarify this message.

Sara also had a personal connection to people with speech disabilities. Before Sara was born, her grandmother was diagnosed with early-onset Parkinson's disease. By the time Sara was a toddler, her grandmother had lost most of her motor capabilities. However, the most challenging adjustment for the family was that Sara's grandmother could not easily communicate with friends or family. During her later years, only a few regular caregivers could understand her voice. It became difficult for anyone else to hear her or build a relationship, including healthcare workers, neighbors, and her beloved grandchildren.

In short, a major draw to the organization was not the technical story unfolding in computing labs, but deep compassion for the people who were neglected or marginalized by their speech. Although the Voiceitt company began with a challenging technical puzzle, their purpose-driven mission led them to the most important business and marketing decisions the company made in its first years. They also learned that the mainstream business community had essentially overlooked this need. Since the 1970s, there have been advancements in speech recognition technology around the world. However, the beneficiaries were almost always people who could speak in standard ways. In fact, using voice to control computers or smart devices had been widely popularized by scientists, film makers, and fiction writers for decades. ("Open the pod bay doors, HAL," being just one example of a human-computer exchange.[6]) But when Amazon and Apple came out with their voice products in the 2010s, most people thought the biggest challenges were solved.

"People believed that Alexa had addressed the major speech recognition issues," recalls Sara Smolley, Vice President of Strategic Partnerships. "But Alexa and Siri *marginalized* the members of numerous communities that had non-standard speakers. The problem was that mainstream speech recognition tools had limited flexibility when it came to processing non-standard voice patterns"[7] (italics added).

A range of medical conditions can impact speech, as do physical disabilities, neurological disorders, and physical changes that come with aging. The practical consequence is that family members and aides often need to verbally translate for people who cannot be understood. In many cases, this ad-hoc translation process is frustrating or unsuccessful, and people with communication disabilities are silenced by their inability to verbalize in standard ways. Yet many with communication challenges *can* verbalize, just in patterns that are unique to the individual. Most non-standard speakers have regular mental abilities, but no way to express their thoughts verbally. Like anyone, non-standard speakers have interests, hopes, and dreams they want to express.

Voiceitt's Speech Recognition Technology

The team at Voiceitt realized that, paradoxically, the rise of new voice technologies had *increased* the sense of isolation for many, because only those who can use standard voice input schemes can use voice communication tools on desktop computers, laptops, tablets, and smartphones, as well as the voice-activated systems in automobiles, phone systems, and other technologies.

Voiceitt began to study the problem in interdisciplinary ways, establishing a community of speech language pathologists, occupational therapists, clinical stakeholders, healthcare administrators, people with speech disabilities, and families. The team listened carefully to each member of the community. This comprehensive approach created an essential feedback loop, so that Voiceitt's engineers would truly focus on the needs of the community in their product design. This removed assumptions about how the product *should work* from the point of view of a person with typical speech patterns.

The Voiceitt underlying core speech recognition technology is available as a consumer application and an Application Programming Interface (API), which enables deeper, direct, and seamless technology integration to assist people with speech disabilities, disorders, and impairments. The Voiceitt consumer application, launched in 2023, is available to consumers with disabilities through Voiceitt's reseller partners. It translates atypical speech so that it can be more easily understood by people *and* automated voice assistants, such as Alexa or Siri. The Voiceitt application is browser-based software that works on any device. It accomplishes its work by learning how each person communicates during a training period, allowing the software to adapt to the user's unique pronunciation. The device's speaker and microphone are put to work in this process, along with custom algorithms that employ machine learning and AI. The application is entirely hands-free. It also integrates with third-party applications, including essential AI productivity tools (ChatGPT) and videoconferencing software. Voiceitt announced a unique integration with Alexa in 2020 and an integration with Webex in 2023. (Amazon and Cisco are investors in Voiceitt, as are two other industry leaders, Microsoft and AARP.)

The Voiceitt application specifically addresses the problem that occurs when a mainstream voice product, such as a smart speaker or captioning system, does not understand a person's unique speech patterns. Using machine learning and voice processing, Voiceitt monitors the user's speech, translates words or sounds as needed, and shares the information directly with the device or software. In this way, someone with a disability can perform basic tasks independently, whether it's turning on lights, starting or stopping music, activating digital equipment, or participating fully in a work call. The impact can be powerful and immediate for Voiceitt users, family members, and care givers. Importantly, Voiceitt gives users a sense of agency and independence, allowing family members more freedom to manage other tasks.

Together, Voiceitt's products serve not only the people with non-standard speech, but the entire community network. "This is not an individual disease," writes Sara Smolley. "For us, the 'customer' is the entire family, social organizations, and the community. This includes healthcare systems, schools, hospitals, and community organizations. At Voiceitt, the customer is not one person, it's an entire community." [8]

Building on this emphasis, Voiceitt has sought to forge strategic relationships that benefit entire communities, not just individuals. This includes the State of Tennessee's Department of Intellectual and Developmental Disabilities (DIDD), which partnered with Voiceitt to test speech technologies in a variety of community settings. The Karten Network in the United Kingdom was also an early adopter of Voiceitt's speech technology, and the company has received numerous endorsements from community partners in Israel, Europe, the UK, and the United States. The list of corporate and foundation sponsors includes AARP, Cisco, the Disability Opportunity Fund, and Microsoft Corporation.

Voiceitt is organized as a private sector social impact organization that fits the "tech for good" company profile we outlined in Chapter 2. They are a lean social enterprise designed to develop and scale effective technology for a socially beneficial cause. Voiceitt is also an excellent example of a purpose-driven company that emphasizes empathy, compassion, and community involvement in everything that they do. The organization shares its Why using mission-oriented goals that serve as a guide to decision making and employee behavior. We list their priorities here as a set of operating principles for any tech for good company that operates to benefit individuals and communities.

Voiceitt's Mission Priorities

1. Our success is measured in how we serve our clients and the families that support them.
2. Towards this end, how many partnerships have we established to magnify the impact of our work?
3. How successful have we been at integrating our technical systems into platforms that are already in use?
4. How many clinicians and healthcare teams recommend our products to clients?
5. Are we perceived as an inclusive organization that advocates for the needs of others? What is the best way to improve our advocacy efforts? [9]

Systemic Funding for Disabilities

The United Nations defines disability as *a long-term physical, mental, intellectual or sensory impairment that may hinder a person's full participation in society on an equal basis with others.* [10]

According to the World Health Fund, 1 billion people in the world have a disability using this definition. However, despite their prevalence, many people with disabilities are still marginalized by communities or left with inadequate products or services. Negative perceptions about those with disabilities are routinely passed along by the media, and programs that serve people with these needs are generally under-resourced.

In our opinion, the disability community is experiencing a compassion crisis. Before we can make headway on this issue, we need social strategies that will help businesses and communities develop empathy and understanding. This multifaceted engagement needs to happen before fundraising or revenue-generation campaigns. Deep listening, storytelling, and shared experiences will be the most powerful tools to do this work.

The United Nations has done essential work by developing 17 Sustainable Development Goals (SDGs) to improve social and economic conditions around the world. However, there is no SDG specifically related to disabilities. The logic here is that because the impact of disabilities on society is so large, the multifaceted issue is best addressed through more than one SDG. Currently, ten of the 17 SDGs have conditions and goals that are tracked separately for people with disabilities. (In other words, the data relating to these SDGs is disaggregated, making it more open to quantitative study.) Another way to think about this is that within vulnerable population groups, there are people *with* disabilities and those *without* disabilities. When people have a disability, social and economic challenges often weigh heavier on them than people who are typically abled. For example, children are especially vulnerable to poverty, diseases, and the impact of war and violence. When a child is disabled, along with other challenges, their life is especially challenging. Women are also a vulnerable population group, but when women are poor, under-educated, threatened by war, *and disabled*, their opportunities are even more circumscribed. People who are 65 and older will represent nearly 20 percent of the U.S. population by 2030, and more than a third of them will have at least one disability.[11] In short, disability is intersectional with other issues, such as age, gender, race, educational attainment, and economic status. This is how the condition has become hidden from view and relatively neglected in policy decisions.

In 2013, Matt Cherry recognized the issues involved and decided to do something about them. Matt is a British citizen from Manchester, England. He and his wife have twin daughters that were born in 2006. Both were diagnosed with autism spectrum disorders, which affect how they interact with others, communicate, and learn.

One is almost completely nonverbal. The girls also have exceptional musical gifts, including perfect pitch and the sensory ability known as synesthesia, in which two or more senses are perceived to blend or overlap. (In their case, they often see colors when they hear music. For example, when Middle C is played on the piano, one of the girls sees the color blue.)

Matt and his wife realized they had some work to do to understand their children's gifts and challenges. The couple began to do research on communication disabilities and how they are managed in social and educational settings. This research task proved challenging, both in the UK and the family's new home in the San Francisco Bay Area. The Cherrys learned that thousands of families struggle to find clear, up-to-date information about the diagnosis, treatment, and support of people with autism spectrum disorders. In addition, they learned that funding for programs that assist families and community members is inequitably distributed. In California, the Cherrys' new home state, the family had access to numerous healthcare and accessibility options. However, the services were not well coordinated, and in many locations, there were major gaps. The situation was worse in many of the neighboring states, and globally, autism spectrum disorders are not uniformly diagnosed and treated. Old stereotypes about autism abound in books, television, and popular media. As a general rule, communication disabilities remain a "hidden" or misdiagnosed problem.

Matt Cherry decided that he would turn his passion for this issue into a vocation. In 2017, he took a job as the development director for a Bay Area nonprofit that supports the families of children with disabilities. The organization's goal is to provide education and parent-to-parent support free of charge to the families of children with any kind of disability. In 2021, Cherry became the Director of Philanthropy at a larger nonprofit organization called Ability Central, a foundation that focuses comprehensively on communication challenges, such as hearing, vision, and speech disabilities. The organization's mission is to serve as a resource, convener, and educator working collaboratively to ensure that people who are Deaf, disabled, or neurodivergent can communicate and access information.[12]

Ability Central is headquartered in Oakland, California, but it supports nonprofit work across the state related to communication disabilities. It is the philanthropic wing of the nonprofit California Communications Access Foundation (CCAF). Their activities are targeted on three impact areas. The first is supporting individuals and families who are currently working through communication challenges. Their objective is to make the world more accessible for all people with disabilities. This makes them the only organization in the State of California that is dedicated to addressing *all* communication challenges, rather than just one or two disorders. The Ability Central team manages a website that provides information about what communication disabilities are and how they can be addressed. They also aggregate data from other sources, such as X4i.org, which tracks hundreds of organizations that help people with communication challenges. Using the Ability Central Portal, families can locate organizations that support Deaf and disabled groups, including clients that are blind, neurodiverse, or have speech or mobility issues.

The second impact area that Ability Central is funding is innovative social impact organizations that are creating value in this space. Initiated in 2010, the Philanthropy program awards funding to nonprofit and educational organizations in California that support the communication needs of Californians of all ages with disabilities. Typically, a total of $1 million per year is distributed to innovation partners via direct financial grants. This allows Ability Central to scale its mission by encouraging others to work toward shared goals. The organization believes that communication is a fundamental human right, and they strive to foster trust building in the face of differences that often separate groups. Ability Central has recently supported Autism Society Inland Empire, Disability Voices United, Noah Homes, Painted Brain, San Diego Pride, and Society for the Blind.

Ability Central is a nonprofit organization that functions like a charitable foundation. The organization supports *other* nonprofits and social impact initiatives that service the community. This makes Ability Central a unique partner in the funding ecosystem for disability services and support. As part of this responsibility, Ability Central has taken on a final task: advocacy. The organization plays a convening role in connecting families to other groups, including socially focused businesses and government agencies. The firm provides news and information, and encourages families to attend community events and participate in consumer advocacy. Ability Central also advocates for accessible design in consumer products and services, especially the computer products used by people with communication disabilities. Matt Cherry writes:

There has never been more opportunity in the user experience (UX) field, because new technical systems are coming out that have the potential to really help people with disabilities. However, often a new tech tool can also present a communication barrier. For example, a new mobile computing tool that requires users to interact with their hands will alienate disabled users who need voice-operated solutions. We try to advocate with industry partners before this happens to promote accessible design in the commercial electronics space.[13]

Ability Central's parent organization, the CCAF, also plays a highly visible role in California's communication-services community. Each year, CCAF receives between $15 and $20 million from the State of California as a service provider to manage the state's telephone access (TTY) program for hearing-impaired callers. This money is set aside by the state legislature annually to provide communication access for Deaf and hard-of-hearing people. In 1990, Title IV of the Americans with Disabilities Act (ADA) required that these services be made available to every state and territory in the U.S. The system was not originally Internet based, but was conceived to work through standard phone systems and relay services. When the telephone access system is engaged, an electronic communication assistant translates voice transmissions to text and displays them on a display device attached to the phone line. This allows a hearing-impaired person to see what another caller has said.

CCAF is responsible for running this service in the State of California, and it employs over 100 people across the state to do this work via 711 calls. Over time, the organization developed a dedicated endowment to launch Ability Central as its philanthropic arm, running the information portal and grant-making programs. This creative arrangement supports an important government-mandated program, while helping social entrepreneurs who are creating important products and services. Ability Central is providing crucial leadership for a collection of issues that need more visibility. They use their *social capital* to raise awareness about communication disabilities, engage in rich storytelling, and foster greater empathy and compassion in the community.

Finding Your "Why"

One of our favorite inspirational authors is Simon Sinek, a business writer best known for the leadership book *Start with Why* (2009).[14] Sinek believes that it is relatively easy for a business owner to explain *what* they do, or even *how* they do it. But few can clearly articulate *why* their business or organization does what they do. Sinek concludes that discovering a purpose-driven Why takes considerable effort. Starting a business is not simply about money or profit—these are the important *results* of business activity. Instead, a Why is more like the central purpose, cause, or belief that inspires you and those around you to engage in the world of work.[15]

Sinek's focus on why we do what we do is especially important for social impact organizations and the employees who work in them. When you have a clear Why, it can serve as a regular guide to decision making and goal setting. A Why can also help employees to solicit community input, set priorities, and build a clear brand and message.

A business leader who exemplifies this approach is Erica Cole, a social entrepreneur who started an adaptable clothing company as a college student at the University of Iowa. In 2018, Erica lost the lower part of her right leg in an automobile crash. After recovering, she needed to adapt to life with a prosthetic. One of the first decisions Erica had to make was how to buy suitable clothing, because her pants no longer fit in the same way. (At first, she typically wore sweat pants that were three times larger than her usual size.)

Fortunately, Erica knew how to operate a sewing machine, and she had experience making her own clothing. Drawing on the skills that she learned designing costumes for theater productions, she began to alter jeans and other outfits so that they fit over her bulky prosthetic. She also recognized that amputees put different stresses on their clothes than non-disabled people do. Erica reinforced the seams and made other alterations to make her pants fit better. Gradually, the word got out that she was making attractive clothing that was also comfortable and practical. Erica took on additional alteration work to support people in the community who were using prosthetics, and many found her designs to be much better than off-the-shelf clothing.

Erica Cole was still a college student at the University of Iowa, studying chemistry and planning a career in science. However, her interactions with people who had different clothing needs had ignited a spark. After some encouragement, she entered an innovation competition called IdeaStorm at the University of Iowa's Pappajohn Entrepreneurial Center. The program is an entry-level pitch competition that encourages students to develop innovative ideas and propose them to others. A panel of judges reviews the competition and selects winners. Erica proposed a company that designs and manufactures adaptable clothing for people with disabilities and limited dexterity. At the end of the 2019 contest, Erica was one of the IdeaStorm winners.

No Limbits and *Shark Tank*

Erica finished her chemistry degree and completed an internship at the Los Alamos National Laboratory, but decided that her career path needed to trend in a different direction. She launched a Kickstarter campaign to raise money for No Limbits, her newly named business. This initial funding helped her to develop a business plan and enroll in an accelerator program for retail startups run by Target Corporation. Erica learned that the fashion industry was still largely traditional, focusing on straight or athletic body types. Although some progress had been made in designs for typical body types, the effort did not extend to customers with disabilities. Erica also learned a lot about manufacturing. As a seamstress, he knew how to make a pair of jeans. But she did not know how to create industrial designs, prototypes, inventory management systems, or supply chain software. The Target business incubator helped her with all of these skills, and convinced her that No Limbits had a unique business story and market opportunity.

After Erica participated in the Target accelerator program, she moved to Richmond, Virginia to participate in another business incubator called Lighthouse Labs. Over three months, entrepreneurs receive startup funds, mentoring, and the support of a cohort. While she was there, Erica received an email from a scout connected to the television show *Shark Tank*. The producers of the reality show had seen Erica's pitch video on YouTube, and they wondered if she would like to apply to be in an upcoming episode? Erica said, "Yes!" and after several months, she was invited to pitch her adaptive clothing concept to the show's cohort of business advisors (the "Sharks"), who offered their usual encouragement, criticism, and advice to contestants. On April 1, 2022, Erica's *Shark Tank* episode finally aired on television, and the public learned that No Limbits had received $100,000 in funding from Mark Cuban and Emma Grede in exchange for 10 percent equity in the company. The organization was on its way.

It was now time to hire employees and create a line of products. In December, 2022, No Limbits announced that an additional $1.4 million had been raised by a handful of small investors to support this work through a second "seed" round of private investment. The funders were Georgetown's Halcyon Angels, New York's Disability Opportunity Fund, Mark Cuban, and Emma Grede. Charles Hammerman of the Disability Opportunity Fund wrote, "No Limbits has a clear understanding of who the company serves and how they will support the disability community with adaptive clothing that is attractive and comfortable. We are thrilled to support this new business."[16]

Erica's company used its financial resources to hire a small number of product designers and business employees to create core adaptive clothing lines and bring them to market. Like many of the companies described in this book, they started small with experienced employees who worked remotely and performed over-lapping roles. Anna Peshock became the company's lead product designer. Anna has experience in the healthcare and apparel industries and a Master of Science degree in Medical Device Innovation from the University of Minnesota-Twin Cities. She is skilled in user-centered design, Agile methodology, prototyping, and soft goods production. Bethany Marvel, another product designer at No Limbits, is an upper extremity amputee and occupational therapist with ten years of experience working with amputees. Bethany also represents the company in healthcare clinics around the country, encouraging physicians and therapists to recommend the products to patients and their families who don't know where to find accessible clothing.

The Covid-19 pandemic was an extremely challenging time to open a manufacturing business that relied on retail sales as a main source of its revenues. However, in 2022 and 2023, No Limbits released several adaptive clothing lines that gained the attention of major clothing retailers. No Limbits began with their Khaki and denim jeans line, designed for people with prosthetics, leg braces, knee braces, ankle-foot orthoses, and lymphedema. During Fall 2022, the team also introduced their innovative wheelchair pants design, with unique styling, zippers, pockets, and stitching. The wheelchair pants were highly reviewed and carefully promoted through video ads that showed male and female models having fun and discussing the products.

During Summer 2023, No Limbits introduced a special clothing line for customers with sensory processing disorders, including "no-tag" tees, comfortable tops, and attractive jackets. The company's website (https://no-limbits.com) presented both ordering information and inspiring stories about customers thriving with confidence and independence despite sensory challenges or disabilities. No Limbits is also a woman-owned business with many employees who are amputees or creators with disabilities or limited dexterity. This makes it clear that No Limbits is on a mission to change the public perception of people with disabilities or sensory challenges. Each employee is personally connected to the No Limbits brand and its aspirational mission, which aligns the life experience of employees with the needs and desires of customers.

On March 8, 2023 (International Women's Day), Erica Cole was pictured on the giant digital display board in front of Nasdaq Tower in Times Square (New York City), celebrating her completion of the Nasdaq Milestone Makers Program, a final startup mentoring program. Erica was 26 years old at the time. Erica described the honor in this way:

Less than 2% of venture funding goes to women founders. Over the past few years of building No Limbits, I've felt like an outsider even more than I did in science. It's hard not to notice [the lack of women], and it's hard not to wonder if I can really make it as a founder. Yet I can point to every single success we've had as being a direct result of a powerful woman leaving the door open behind her. To all the incredible women who have helped me on this journey, thank you. One day I hope to leave some doors open too.[17]

Like many successful startups, mentorship from others had a leading role in the success of No Limbits. The company greatly benefited from the influence of Mark Cuban, Emma Grede, and Todd Stockbauer, an advisor on brand marketing and startup strategy. According to Erica, the *Shark Tank* investors ask for updates every week, and they often reply in days with additional advice or connections. Grede is particularly experienced with the clothing industry and helped to launch the Good American brand with Khloé Kardashian to empower women of all sizes through high-quality designs. Erica Cole is also seen as a leader in adaptive clothing design, with nationwide accounts in retailers like Walmart.

It remains to be seen how far No Limbits will go in their mission to serve neglected and marginalized communities through apparel. However, we highlight this example of a purpose-driven company to inspire future business leaders who aspire to make a meaningful difference in the social impact sector. Finding your Why can be both personally satisfying and a step toward making the world a better place. The sector is abundant with these opportunities. When asked about how she motivates employees to help the company on its mission, Erica Cole responded:

You have to make sure the people you work with have the tools that they need to succeed, and that there are clearly defined goals and objectives. The other challenge: the people I've hired are experts in their field and know more than I do. I have to stay out of their way but make sure that they're on a path that's aligned with the mission and vision of the company.[18]

Immerse Yourself

Embedding purpose into projects is built around the core insight that to solve meaningful problems you need to step into another's shoes, understand their lives, and meet challenges with new perspectives.

Immersing yourself in another setting not only opens you up to creative possibilities but allows you to leave behind outdated ways of thinking. This is the core vision of purpose-driven innovation, inspired by empathy and community engagement.

Many social impact organizations assume that their mission is clear to the public and needs little explanation. An agency that supplies assistive devices such as wheelchairs or braille materials to people who are disabled might seem like an obvious example of a purpose-driven organization. However, if employees do not know exactly *why* their clients need assistive devices and *how* these devices will change their lives, the company will have a hard time communicating their message.

To risk repetition, we believe that a carefully articulated Why is more than justifying an operating budget on moral or religious grounds. A Why can clarify a new company's core values and priorities. The commitment also functions as a kind of ethical "North Star," which enlivens and guides organizations as they pursue success. *Innovation by Design* authors Thomas Lockwood and Edgar Papke write about this kind of alignment when they observe,

> The simple truth is that, for any organization to be innovative requires it to have a shared set of ideals … If members are in alignment with an organization's purpose for existence, they will be more engaged and more motivated in how they think and act.[19]

In this chapter, we've met three dynamic leaders who have provided this kind of alignment in the social impact sector. Danny Weissberg, Matt Cherry, and Erica Cole each became inspired to help others through their personal experience with community members who had to work to overcome challenges. The companies that they operate and inspire are now scaling their ideas to help many others.

What work do you feel called to do? How can you share this vision with others?

Notes

1 For the United Way's current mission statement, see www.unitedway. org/our-impact/mission.
2 Research on leadership and compassion is summarized in the article "Purpose is Everything" published by Deloitte Insights (October 2019); see www.deloitte.com/au/en/our-thinking/insights/topics/ marketing-sales/global-marketing-trends/2020/purpose-driven- companies.html. Accessed December 5, 2023. For useful examples about how to promote purpose-driven culture in organizations,

see Akhtar Badshah, *Purpose Mindset: How Microsoft Inspires Employees and Alumni to Change the World* (New York: Harper-Collins Leadership, 2020).

3   See Anita Baggio, Valeria Bundinich, Nora Gardner, and Fernande Raine, "Answering Society's Call: A New Leadership Imperative," *McKinsey Quarterly* (November 2019); www.mckinsey.com/capabilities/people-and-organizational-performance/our-insights/answering-societys-call-a-new-leadership-imperative. Accessed December 5, 2023.

4   The authors thank Danny Weissberg and Sara Smolley for sharing their stories and recent information about Voiceitt's products. (Email correspondence on December 12 and 13, 2023.)

5   For recent research about compassion and useful definitions from a range of disciplines, see *The Oxford Handbook of Compassion Science* (Oxford: Oxford University Press, 2022), 3.

6   This memorable scene between Dave and HAL (the on-board flight computer) is part of Stanley Kubrick's *2001: A Space Odyssey* (Metro-Goldwyn-Mayer, 1968). The film is based on Arthur C. Clarke's 1951 short story "The Sentinel."

7   "Interview with Sara Smolley and Dr. Rachel Levy," *Equal Inspired* 10 (February 22, 2023). Video recording available at: www.youtube.com/watch?v=XK9SmD8t-6U. Accessed December 5, 2023.

8   "Interview with Sara Smolley," February 22, 2023.

9   "Interview with Sara Smolley," February 22, 2023.

10 United Nations, "Convention on the Rights of Persons with Disabilities", Article 1: Purpose. www.un.org/development/desa/disabilities/convention-on-the-rights-of-persons-with-disabilities/article-1-purpose.html. Accessed December 5, 2023.

11 Disability Opportunity Fund, "The Stride Report" (Rockville Centre, NY, February 2023), 3.

12 For the company mission statement, see https://aboutus.abilitycentral.org. Accessed December 5, 2023.

13 Matt Cherry interview (via Zoom), April 27, 2023. Michael Halvorson and Shelly Cano Kurtz interviewers.

14 Simon Sinek, *Start with Why: How Great Leaders Inspire Everyone to Take Action* (New York: Portfolio/Penguin, 2009).

15 Sinek, *Start with Why*, 39.

16 Phone conversation with Charles D. Hammerman, Shelly Cano Kurtz, and Michael Halvorson (March 27, 2023).

17 Shalene Gupta, "This 27-year-old CEO wants to build an adaptive clothing empire," Fast Company (June 26, 2023). www.fastcompany.com/90912671/erica-cole-founder-no-limbits-interview-adaptive-clothing-shark-tank. Accessed December 5, 2023.

18 Gupta, "CEO wants adaptive clothing empire."

19 Thomas Lockwood and Edgar Papke, *Innovation by Design: How Any Organization Can Leverage Design Thinking to Produce Change, Drive New Ideas, and Deliver Meaningful Solutions* (Newburyport, MA: Career Press, 2018), 198.

5 Design Thinking for Changemakers

The most successful social enterprises seek to enable changemaking across the entire organization, accelerating and deepening social impact. This collaborative work can help organizations unlock new and untapped markets, build momentum in teams, and establish a competitive advantage for social impact initiatives.

But *wanting* to make a positive impact is not the same thing as achieving it.

In this chapter, we focus on the "How" of creating social and economic value in organizations. We introduce *design thinking*, a creative approach to innovation that focuses on assessing community needs, building effective teams, and rapidly testing ideas so that they can be adopted and embraced. Design thinking was popularized in the 2010s by organizations like IDEO in Silicon Valley, which promoted its use through seminars, workshops, and innovative publications.[1] Despite its use in leading technology firms, however, design thinking is still relatively unknown in the social impact sector. In the following sections, we explore its use and show how design thinking can raise awareness about social and environmental challenges, test assumptions, generate new ideas, and bring new insights to market. You'll learn the five stages of design thinking and how this strategic mindset can be used to mobilize resources and energize stakeholders. You'll also learn about human-centered design (HCD), a methodology that applies design thinking principles to community-based challenges that are intimately connected to people and the ecosystems they flourish in.[2] Our featured case studies include a U.S.-based computer literacy initiative, a community rainwater system in West Africa, and a civic engagement project for young people in the Pacific Northwest.

A Human-Centered Approach

In Chapter 1, we defined social impact work as *activity that seeks to improve the well-being of individuals and communities by addressing social and economic issues such as poverty, inequality, access to*

DOI: 10.4324/9781003465669-5

education, and healthcare. This work can take a range of forms, including advocacy, philanthropy, bringing new products or services to market, and more. In each of these contexts, the goal of social impact activity is to create positive change in society through actions that address the *root causes* of social and environmental problems.

The goal of design thinking is to start this journey by discovering the underlying context of social and environmental challenges in a systematic way. Design thinking is an iterative process that can be used for any type of planning or business activity, but the practice is especially well suited to social innovation projects that are centered on addressing unmet needs within specific communities or comprehensive, multifactorial problems like sustainability challenges. In these contexts, design thinking is often associated with *changemaking*, because to support vulnerable groups or fix inefficient practices it is sometimes necessary to challenge the status quo. Design thinking also helps organizations to identify constraints and manage resources efficiently. It's a human-centered approach to problem solving rooted in empathy and compassion. It's deeply concerned with *how* products and services are used and *who* will use them.

In the past, the words "innovative design" were often used to signal the arrival of new consumer goods in the marketplace that were fashionable, stylish, or sleek. Most people associate award-winning design with retail products like furniture, designer glasses, or the latest smartphone. But the last decade has witnessed a dramatic expansion in what the terms "design" and "innovation" mean in the world of business. IDEO, a design and consulting firm located in Palo Alto, California, popularized the expectation that breakthrough ideas—whether for innovative consumer products or public initiatives—should be the result of a design process that puts people first, perceives design problems as opportunities, and recognizes design constraints as a regular feature of business. Design thinking using this approach is exemplified by creative ideation or "brainstorming," testing concepts rapidly, and refining procedures to create *value* in organizations. Most importantly, design thinking is grounded in empathy and compassion for others. Former IDEO CEO Tim Brown writes, "Design thinking taps into capacities we all have but that are overlooked by more conventional problem-solving practices. It is not only human-centered; it is deeply human in and of itself."[3]

Understanding design thinking as a *process* can help social innovators learn what it means to create value in a range of contexts. Although there are many stereotypes about the solitary inventor toiling away in his or her lab to perfect some new gadget or invention, the reality is that innovation challenges are best solved in teams, following procedures that stitch together existing knowledge about a subject, adequate financial resources, and diverse workgroups that improve on initial ideas using a range of skills. Although Dr. Emmet Brown worked on his own to build a spectacular "DeLorean time machine" in the blockbuster *Back to the Future* (1985), a more realistic model for innovation is depicted in the film *Hidden Figures* (2016), which portrays a range of inventors, engineers, and knowledge workers collaborating to enable the first NASA space flights in the early 1960s. This real-life team of innovators included mission planners, mathematicians, scientists, engineers, astronauts, and a group of relatively unknown women "human computers" who calculated trajectories for the missions by hand. Powerfully, *Hidden Figures* explores how socially marginalized figures often perform essential (if hidden) roles in the innovation process. In short, innovation is a diverse team sport, not an individual activity. The wider the talent pool of contributors, the better the chance for lasting success. Teams with diverse backgrounds bring a variety of skills and perspectives that can translate into greater problem-solving capabilities.

Design thinking is also an *interdisciplinary process* that draws energy and expertise from many different subject areas. At Pacific Lutheran University (PLU), Michael Halvorson teaches design thinking as part of an Innovation Studies program that draws inspiration and expertise from the departments of Art & Design, Business, Communication, Computer Science, Economics, English, History, and Psychology. The program was started in 2016 when a group of faculty, students, and alumni realized that in the business and nonprofit worlds, the skills necessary for developing new ideas typically transcend the academic boundaries found within universities. The Innovation Studies curriculum enables students to integrate their coursework into a rich interdisciplinary framework that emphasizes critical thinking, entrepreneurship, social impact training, and vocational reflection. Fundamental to this education is the concept that design thinking is a creative process that *everyone* can learn. It is a mindset that is useful in nonprofit organizations, government work, higher education, business settings, healthcare, athletics, entertainment, science, and a range of creative endeavors.

The Blessing of Constraints

Fundamental to the design thinking process is understanding what is possible within the limits of available resources, institutional boundaries, time, and other *constraints*. Although it might seem disheartening to think about constraints in a book about innovation, in design thinking, the *limits* of what teams can accomplish are actually hidden blessings. Practical constraints allow innovators to focus their energies on what is realistic and actually needed by communities. For example, if a well-meaning team designs a new automobile that is extremely safe to drive, but is well beyond the budget of most people, what kind of social impact would this safe automobile have in the world? The car's social impact would surely be limited, because the cost would exceed the resources of most people. Wouldn't it be wiser to build most automobiles so that they are safe and affordable? Or to find alternative transportation mechanisms for people that are safer or more efficient than cars?

In design thinking, a common way to discuss the importance of constraints is to create a Venn diagram with overlapping circles that depict the convergence of three variables: *what people actually want* (Desirable), *what is technically possible to create* (Feasible), and *what is sustainable for an organization to implement* (Viable) (see Figure 5.1). This type of diagram is helpful because social innovators need to be reminded that they should (1) create products, services, and campaigns that satisfy the needs of actual communities; (2) stay within the limits of current technological systems and social or institutional values; and (3) build something that is sustainable for an organization to support over the long term.

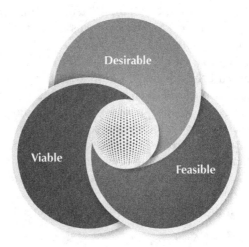

Figure 5.1 Constraints are important in social innovation. At the intersection of Desirable, Feasible, and Viable is a potential sweet spot for a new product or idea.

A Diversity and Inclusion Case Study

For example, the nonprofit organization Code.org was created in 2013 to build learning pathways into computer programming (or computational logic) for people who have never written a program before. Code.org was especially interested in boosting the number of women and underrepresented minorities learning to code in the United States, then learning how to scale these efforts in more global contexts. If the training and learning initiative is successful, it could lead to a more diverse and inclusive workforce, and better hardware and software systems.

However, the organization is severely limited by a number of practical constraints. First, computer science is not a regular part of the middle school or high school curriculum in most school districts in the U.S. It competes with reading, writing, and a number of important scientific subjects, such as biology, chemistry, and physics. Second, the funding required to train new teachers, buy computers and software, and develop a scaffolded approach to learning is beyond all but the wealthiest school districts. Third, computer science is one of the most challenging subjects to teach and learn, especially when students do not have a strong background in mathematics or logic. By its very nature, the curriculum requires small group instruction, long-term mentoring relationships, and years of practice for the best outcomes.

Nonetheless, Code.org was able to create a successful learning system that has had a real impact on education and workforce training or *skilling* initiatives in the U.S. The organization is funded by a large consortium of tech companies, state governments, schools, and individual donors.[4] For a decade, Code.org has worked within financial and structural limits to build and deploy curricula that have been sustainable and enabled millions of women and underrepresented minorities to enter the workforce. The nonprofit's signature event is Hour of Code, an annual programming workshop for students and teachers that celebrates the birthday of computing pioneer Admiral Grace Murray Hopper, born December 9, 1906. From a design thinking point of view, an emphasis on the practical constraints of desirable, feasible, and viable have created a window of opportunity for Code.org. The team designed a solution that supports existing school districts by locating and training new teachers, raising awareness about computer science, and supporting the development of technological infrastructure. Code.org also partnered with sports and entertainment figures to make programming look fun, interesting, and useful.

The Five Design Stages

Finding the intersection among desirable, feasible, and viable is challenging, because each constraint is usually determined by a range of factors. This is why design thinking is a multistage process with methodologies that evaluate or test solutions against real community needs. The five design stages are referred to as Empathy, Define, Ideate, Prototype, and Test (see Figure 5.2). Since IDEO popularized the use of these five stages a decade ago, there have been numerous variations to the design thinking paradigm by practitioners. Some of the models use slightly different terminology to highlight a specific point in the design process. The design framework is meant to be simple for all to learn, but there is considerable complexity beneath it.

Design thinking is also a strategic approach to problem solving, a mindset that distinguishes successful social impact organizations. If you're entering this field, it is likely that you'll encounter this terminology in job interviews, team meetings, and the planning process for new products or initiatives. In particular, tech for good organizations often use design thinking strategies when they develop new technical services or interfaces to hardware or software. Design thinking allows organizations to move from product conception to scaling at a speed that feels rushed for conventional planners. However, the process quickly becomes more concrete with detailed examples, and we provide them in the following sections.

Empathy in Design

The first stage in design thinking is Empathy, which means thinking deeply about the people, communities, and systems that you will

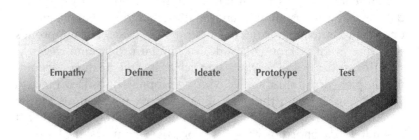

Figure 5.2 The five stages of design thinking: Empathy, Define, Ideate, Prototype, and Test. Although the stages are usually represented as step-by-step or "linear" phases in social innovation models, the stages can also be circular in nature. For example, it is normal to discover during the Prototype stage that the team needs to return to Empathy or Define using insights gained from experimentation.

support with your innovation. As Teresa Chahine advises in her helpful book *Social Entrepreneurship*, it's an innovator's job to immerse themselves in the social challenge that they are tackling.[5] By this, Chahine means that innovators should "get in the middle" of the situation that they are trying to improve, rather than imagining a social or environmental problem from the outside.

Chahine's advice brings up an important point: The problems that social innovators are usually tasked with are not their own. Because of this, it is easy to become myopic or self-centered when you are designing solutions for others, especially when you are imagining the social or cultural context of another person. A common pitfall when designing for others is imagining that your customers have the same business conditions or psychological needs that you do. For example, although Apple's iPhone is a familiar consumer product in the United States, until recently it was almost completely unavailable in India, the most populous country on earth. It would be a mistake for a social innovator to assume that an iOS application would be the best fit for most global markets. The same is true for media content, cultural values, and more rudimentary matters such as how user interfaces are presented in software systems. How often have we seen products that are fun and exciting for teenagers in the U.S. but which fall flat when they are used by older adults or users in global contexts?

The Empathy stage asks us to recognize and understand the perspective of others, working to interact with, and learn from, community members who have a different perspective and worldview. Empathy requires that you step into another person's shoes and focus on your own motivations and blind spots. Design teams need to trust each other in this work and assume that co-workers and stakeholders have good intentions—even when they disagree about customer needs or product strategy. If you look at this stage functionally, Empathy is about learning from one another and discovering service gaps or opportunities where improvements can be made. To achieve this, team members should strive to *observe* how clients do things now, and how they interact with their tools and environment. Social innovators need to understand problems deeply and not simply suggest solutions along the lines of "how we do it here."

IDEO co-founder Tom Kelley describes empathic observation as using the skills of an anthropologist, meaning that it is important to set aside what you think you "know" about a situation and immerse yourself in the cultural world of another. Anthropologists work very hard to look beyond preconceived notions and avoid being judgmental. In the book *The Ten Faces of Innovation*, Kelley mentions how a colleague named Patrice Martin became an exceptionally good observer and design thinker. According to Kelley, Martin enjoyed meeting and talking to people, asking probing questions, and projecting a nonthreatening image to others. Over time, these habits became an intuitive sense about how to listen to clients and uncover stories that reveal "epiphanies" about their needs.[6]

The work of Empathy is best carried out through face-to-face conversation and questioning: "How do young people walk to school in your neighborhood? What do they do after school? What are their biggest hopes, dreams, and needs?" Emphatic research can also be continued through social research methods, including developing surveys or questionnaires, studying government reports, reviewing academic literature, and partnering with philanthropic foundations to analyze data.

In college classrooms, Michael introduces the Empathy stage by asking students to pair up and participate in directed conversations that teach interview and listening skills. The first student initially takes on the role of interviewer, and the second student takes the role of interviewee. The first student then asks the second to describe a community need they have witnessed or experienced recently. While the interviewee speaks, the interviewer listens intently, jots down notes, and refrains from talking. The goal is to listen and watch for body language and facial expressions. The instructor times the students and, after five or six minutes, asks them to reverse roles. The second student then asks the first what community needs they have witnessed or experienced? The goal is not conversation but listening for challenges or problems that might be solved. (If a community-based challenge does not feel like a good fit for your class, select another social or environmentally focused theme.)

During each round of conversation, partners take notes about what they learn from each other. There is then a slightly longer follow-up period in which they ask each other deeper questions about the roots of the problems they have observed. During this phase, interviewers should be encouraged to ask rich journalistic questions beginning with "who," "what," "when," "where," "why," and "how" about what they are observing, trying to understand the underlying issues. After both partners have the opportunity to describe their challenge and follow up with detailed analysis, the entire group reconvenes and discusses shared trends and insights.

If there is an opportunity to continue the listening and learning over multiple days, the instructor or facilitator can arrange for in-depth reading about the subject, including industry reports, quantitative analysis, and academic studies. After this type of preparation, the group will be ready to take their Empathy skills into new settings. Learning how to be an empathetic listener can be rich and rewarding, especially when the goal is speaking face-to-face with community members. Even after a little training, designers can start to engage positively with others, listen in humble, emotive ways, and gather insights about a community and its hopes, dreams, and needs. When teams are prepared in this way, they will be less likely to push their own "solutions" on others, and more skilled at framing conceptual problems or opportunities from a community point of view. The Empathy stage of design thinking is ultimately about gathering information in an impartial way that can be further validated by research, community discussion, and data-centered analysis. (For more information about using data effectively, see Chapter 7.)

A Focus on Teaming

If it isn't obvious already, we believe that effective planning and research is related to effective *teaming*, or working together purposefully as a group, with defined roles and responsibilities. An individual innovator can only discover so much when examining a complex problem. But a focused team of five or six can change the world.

How important is effective teaming? Demonstrating the ability to work well on diverse teams is now considered to be the #1 skill a college graduate can possess to show readiness for employment by U.S. companies.[7] This is because working on complex problems typically requires evaluating multiple perspectives and leveraging different skills, including approaching challenges with interdisciplinary training and expertise. Simply put, corporations want problem solvers who can think, learn, and write in a variety of ways. Although diversity in terms of gender and ethnic identity is important, it is also valuable for people to have training in different dimensions of the human experience. For example, in Chapter 4 we learned that focusing on hidden disabilities can yield important breakthroughs for a company. Considering age and ageism is also an important consideration for design teams. This means including people that are either senior citizens or who understand the needs of people as they age (gerontology). In many tech companies, it is difficult to find designers or engineers who are 55 or older, despite the fact that one-third of the U.S. population will be a senior citizen by the year 2030. Age diversity is a fundamental aspect of holistic human-centered design.

Psychological safety is also important in teams, so that each team member can freely share their perspectives on the needs of others. Successful team leaders emphasize psychological safety by developing a clear structure in the group with roles and responsibilities, and emphasizing interpersonal attributes, such as dependability and trust. Google, a company that is famous for effective teaming, regularly publicizes its vision for psychological safety in workgroups, including a list of characteristics that nurture successful design. The company believes that team members are most satisfied when they know that their work has *meaning* and that they are contributing to projects that will have a *positive impact* on society.

Professor Amy C. Edmondson at Harvard Business School suggests that effective teaming is an especially important factor in innovation and design projects:

> Teaming is a process of bringing together skills and ideas from disparate areas to produce something new—something that no one individual, or even a group in one area of expertise, could do alone. This is why teaming is so crucial to innovation. In some ways, teaming to innovate is the most engaging and rewarding kind of teaming there is.[8]

Capturing Rainwater in West Africa

One of the crucial clarion calls for Empathy in design work comes from the international development community.

In the past, this sector has tended to approach challenges like poverty in Africa without truly empathizing with or understanding the people it is trying to help.[9] Eager to bring pre-developed solutions to communities that could benefit from them, nongovernmental organizations (NGOs) have brought off-the-shelf, commercial solutions designed for a different region to temporarily address the needs of others. Unfortunately, this has sometimes resulted in wasted time, ineffective campaigns, and harm to communities. A collaborative process like the grassroots movement that devised the United Nations Sustainable Development Goals (UN SDGs) has improved community engagement and social impact. It started with listening, clarifying goals and objectives, and involving local partnerships in design projects.

In Thiès, Senegal, modern farmers struggle through the dry season which now stretches to almost nine months of the year in parts of West Africa. In 2022, an international design team developed an innovative rainwater capture system in Senegal to "harvest" rainwater during heavy periods of rain and preserve it, resulting in water stocks that now benefit over 450 households.[10]

This social innovation involves more than preserving water in the community—it also includes monitoring supply inputs and using water in ways that equitably benefit the community. The system increases crop and fruit tree productivity, supports community needs, and allows residents to buy necessary goods like medicine and education for their children. The solution was developed after a careful assessment of community needs, involved community members and partners within the international development community, and is monitored and enhanced by members of the Thiès farming community.

The water problem was highlighted by UN SDG #6: Clean Water and Sanitation. But to address this development goal, social innovators need to put local communities first, working one location at a time to transform inspiration into action. Empathy is the design stage where social innovators deeply listen and understand the needs of others in their local context. After a solution has been found and implemented, it might be possible to extend the reach of (or *scale*) the intervention to other communities. However, it is important to verify that the underlying cause of the problem has been addressed rather than just its symptoms.

Defining Your Problem

The next stage in design thinking is *defining* a problem that needs to be solved. This process takes shape after teams evaluate the information that has been gathered during the Empathy stage and turn it into insights. Remember: You're not just solving your own problem, you're solving the problem of another group or organization. Even if you learned about a social or environmental challenge through careful research, or were drawn to a problem using the UN SDGs, you still need to address a specific challenge through an intervention that will benefit specific individuals. The output of the Define stage is to create one or more problem statements that clearly identify the issue you are trying to address.

Defining a problem is best thought of as a collaborate process. Again, you'll want different insights and perspectives to formulate the problem with appropriate terminology and cultural framing.

Creative "makerspaces" are helpful as a work environment when information from different people is stirred together into a practical solution. An ideal makerspace for social innovation work is a well-lit conference room or meeting space containing white boards, movable chairs, post-it notes, construction paper, markers, cardboard, and other creative supplies. A "what and where" exercise that Michael likes to use to help designers identify problems involves drawing a grid of rows and columns on a movable white board, and then asking team members to use the grid to identify challenges that they discovered while listening to a group describe what they would like to fix or address. Participants are asked to write down five or six common problems as row headings on the left side of the whiteboard. Then designers are asked to identify locations where these problems have surfaced using column headers across the top of the white board. Finally, participants place post-it notes in the grid containing stories about the problems they have noticed, finding in the cells that match the "what" and "where" headers. It may also be helpful to use different marker colors to highlight problem categories, or to draw pictures that convey ideas.

What most design teams discover is that the problems they are trying to solve have specific contexts, and there will be differences of opinion about the underlying causes. Team members will do their best "defining" work when they have something visual to look at. Creating a grid full of stories and other evidence from the community helps move the process along. When the team can talk about social challenges in a tangible way, they go deeper and have an opportunity to share their lived experience.

The output of the Define stage is a written problem definition that the team can agree on and share with others. From the many problems that are discovered and discussed, one short, written definition is helpful because it encapsulates what the group actually believes about a problem and what they aspire to address. The problem definition should be clear and concrete, reflecting the point of view of your group and the community you are designing for. Our complex world has many problems that are worth thinking about. But this problem statement is the one your organization is trying to solve *now*. By agreeing on a problem, you set the stage for ideation, the brainstorming phase where you propose practical solutions.

To prepare a problem statement, narrow your approach by asking journalistic type questions about the evidence. Use who, what, where, when, and why.

Sample questions you might ask to prepare a problem statement include:

- **Who is experiencing the problem?** Who do you see as the target customer or community that is experiencing a challenge right now?
- **What is the problem?** Based on your initial observations, what are the main problems or "pain points" that come up over and over for the community you are trying to help? What task is the group trying to accomplish? What makes the task inefficient now? What is standing in the community's way?
- **Where does the problem usually present itself?** Where are the people living or working? (In what physical or digital space?) What is the context for the group that faces this problem?
- **When did the problem arise?** When did community members first notice it? When did other people become interested in this issue? Has it happened elsewhere?
- **Why does it matter?** Why is it important that this particular problem be solved? What benefit would a solution bring to the user, the community, or the organization?

With these insights in hand, it's time to formalize your design challenge by writing a problem statement. If possible, your problem should be just one to three sentences long. (You can write down additional notes later.) Following IDEO's lead, this is the format we recommend for a problem statement:

_____ needs a way to _____.

Surprisingly, _____.

You'll notice that the model presented here asks you to identify a person or group, an action that they need to do, and something surprising or unusual that is blocking them.

Here's an example. Imagine that a group of school teachers, parents, government officials, and community leaders are meeting to discuss the challenges that currently face school districts in the community. After careful listening and fact finding, a community group forms to explore possible solutions. In one of the sessions, a respected teacher presents a government study that links nutrition to students' thinking skills, behavior, and health. In a follow-up conversation, several community members mention that they have heard about this research, and they want to determine how student nutrition might be improved locally. The Define stage is the place where this type of insight might be put into words that highlight the specific nature of the problem and the elements of a solution.

One way to write the problem definition for this hypothetical case could be:

> <u>Our community</u> **needs a way** to <u>improve the quality of food that students receive during the week. We believe that success in the classroom is related to good nutrition for all students.</u> **Surprisingly,** <u>we have found that healthy food options do exist in the community, but many of our students don't take advantage of them</u>.

This hypothetical statement gathers data from community conversation and research. It includes information about a problem that has been identified, including the belief that nutrition and student success are linked. It also identifies a situation that is not working in the community—students appear to have access to food, but they aren't eating what's best for them. Also note that a complete "solution" is not presented, just the problem. But it is a specific statement that seeks an intervention. What is most useful is if the statement represents the beliefs of most of the people in the community. (In other words, the problem statement should be generally agreed upon, not just the idea of one person.)

It can take a lot of work to write a good problem statement. However, it can also be fun work, especially when everyone feels included and listened to. Detailed problem statements are particularly helpful. For example, compare the following statements. Each successfully identifies a problem, but the second and third statements are the most detailed, and more likely to spur productive ideation sessions in the coming days.

> **Good:** "Our students need a way to eat better during the day, and we want to feed them nutritious things."
>
> **Better:** "Our high school students need better nutrition and a way to find the food that they can eat near where they live. They also need to learn that good food matters."
>
> **Best:** "The high school students in our community struggle to eat healthy meals during the week because they get up early, work long hours, and have limited shopping choices. Moreover, some live where nutritious food is unavailable. This active group needs options for meals and snacks that they can locate near them. They also need to believe that nutritious food matters."

Defining a problem means to take insights and observations from a community and turn them into a written statement that summarizes who is having a problem and what needs to change. A compact problem statement requires some nuance and deliberation, because everyone will not agree on just what the challenge is or who is inconvenienced by it. In fact, "stakeholders who can't agree on the problem" has recently been identified as one of the major challenges confronting leaders and community members who are designing solutions in the social impact sector.[11] However, if your research is based on community engagement and empathy, it is likely that you'll begin to spot trends when you ask journalistic questions that synthesize insights and ask who, what, where, and why. Remember that defining a problem is narrowing the challenge you are identifying and focusing on a specific attribute of the problem that a large group of people can agree with. This is your starting point for social innovation.

Ideation for Impact

The Ideation phase of design thinking, popularly called "brainstorming", is the time for the design team to "open wide" again and create a range of possible *solutions* to the problem or issue that you have identified. Ideation means *to generate a wide range of ideas in graphical or written form that have the potential to solve a problem that has been identified by a team or community*. Ideation is a creative act of synthesis and solution building, focusing on what could be, not the countless obstacles that may get in the way.[12]

Research shows that the best ideation sessions are those that take place in groups that trust each other and recognize the value of each member's perspective. Ideation should not be the first activity that a new group or team does together because it can feel awkward to think conceptually or take a social risk. Ideation is also not a place for the *devil's advocate*, a person who voices one negative opinion after the next, in order to test the merits of an idea. The time will come for concerns about feasibility and viability. (See Chapter 8 and the requirements for scaling.) But in its early stages, ideation is about *cultivating creativity* and setting up procedures that encourage individual contributors to brainstorm. Leaders should try to boost the *quantity* of ideas, encouraging every team member to participate, and developing systems to capture what is suggested.

By the time a design team gets to ideation, they will have compiled lots of information about clients and their needs. This information should be organized into lists that summarize community strengths, challenges, and opportunities. Draw on your earlier work to recall common pain points, reviewing "what and where" grids about how problems arise, and why this particular design challenge matters. Flag key insights about the problem and try to embed insights into possible solutions. Your goal is to synthesize your findings and look for common patterns.

Ideation initially involves writing lists of ideas or creating rudimentary drawings that capture elements of a solution. Ask yourself questions like "How might we solve this problem?" Then record hunches proposed by team members. Be as visual as possible, using white boards, story boards, computer-assisted design tools, post-it notes, photos, and other visual tools. Resist the temptation to use AI tools initially, because the system will not be trained to address the specific needs of your community. Organize and record your ideas, so that connections become apparent as new ideas are generated. Consider asking your design team to develop five ideas each day for several days about the design challenge. Be sure to capture "crazy ideas" each day, as well—these proposals keep the creative juices flowing, lighten the mood, and can sometimes contain the seeds of a fantastic, unique solution.

One way to measure the pace of ideation is to keep track of *ideas* that surface. Write down each possible solution on a white board, using a one-word solution or a short phrase to capture the insight. Try to generate as many ideas as possible, writing each idea on the board. Help team members to develop their ideas, using phrases like "and" or "which leads to" to build on concepts they introduce. Be light-hearted and playful, encouraging truly outrageous or unexpected ideas, which occasionally contain an insight that can be helpful. ("You know, that's actually a great idea.")

In professional situations, we find that the best facilitators don't present the ideas themselves, because their influence can sometimes stifle creative conversation. Instead, leaders find ways to *extend* ideation sessions after the initial enthusiasm is gone or team members feel as if they've reached an impasse. They establish simple rules like "one person should speak at a time" and "let's agree to not judge other people's ideas." The most important guideline is to stay focused on the problem statement that has been defined. Remind the group that among the many problems that *could* be solved, we are working on the one that has been *defined* by a community that is experiencing it. "How can we help them?"

IDEO has popularized the use of conceptual models called *frameworks* to support the ideation process. In addition to writing down lists of ideas, it can be very helpful to build a conceptual framework that visually represents important relationships. For example, if the problem is improving a process, like how people recycle paper and food containers in the workplace, creating a *journey map* will allow you to visualize the recycling process from beginning to end (see Figure 5.3). A journey map imagines a customer experience or procedure as though it is a visual excursion on a map, with stages and stops. If you display such a map during an ideation session, team members can suggest ways to simply or optimize the process. Likewise, a *relational map* is a framework that shows how different ideas relate to one another. This ideation tool can help you visualize new ways to connect people or resources, allowing the team to spot unrecognized patterns or synergies and connections among them.

Civic Engagement in Tacoma

The Innovation Studies program at PLU recently co-sponsored a design challenge with South Sound Together, a community organization in Tacoma, Washington, to more fully understand the aspirations of young people related to civic engagement in the region. (Young

Journey Map

Relational Map

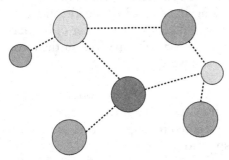

Figure 5.3 Two popular frameworks that support ideation efforts during the design thinking process.

people were defined as residents of the community under 25 years of age). The key questions the group wanted to study were:

- "What about civic engagement appeals to young people in the region?"
- "What are the barriers to civic engagement that young people currently experience?"
- "How could we creatively overcome these barriers?"

Although we used the term "civic engagement" with our clients, we were also curious about the term *citizenship* and its relationship to social impact work. After doing some initial research with Dr. Michael Artime, a political scientist at PLU, we realized there were two popular meanings for the term citizenship in American society, and they were somewhat different. *Duty-based citizenship* has the more traditional meaning, involving shared obligations such as paying taxes, voting, and serving in the military. But *engaged citizenship* reflects newer social norms in America, including being active in the community, helping those worse off, keeping watch on the government, and advocating for change when necessary. So we wondered: Which definition resonates with young people in the Tacoma area today? Did anything about citizenship or civic engagement interest them? If so, how could we support the next generation to take leadership roles in the community?

In this scenario, South Sound Together brought their design challenge to us, along with considerable research they had done about challenges facing young people. This group of leaders was concerned that high schoolers had little time for civic engagement with their schedules, and when they graduated, they were either off to college or busy finding work and starting a career. In their minds, an entire generation was missing out on the opportunity for public service. Our PLU design team followed up with a focus group for students aged 17 to 25 in the Tacoma area. We learned that young people could identify a number of barriers that made it difficult for them to be actively involved in their community. The most pressing barriers were:

1. There is a lack of information about what the community needs are (or how they might help).
2. Young people wanted to help, but they were short on time and had no transportation.
3. The weekly requirements of volunteer work (hours/training) seemed too high.

4. There was an oversaturation of choices (young people didn't know where to begin).
5. Advertisements from organizations seemed tone-deaf to young people or the issues they cared about.
6. Social divisions and the current political climate felt toxic (producing anxiety).

PLU's design team did additional research through community groups in the region, exploring opportunities for networking and engagement in the area. They also met with college students from PLU, Bates Technical College, Tacoma Community College, and University of Washington, Tacoma. In our design rubric, we identified this research as part of the Empathy stage, or getting to know the community we were serving.

Michael acted as the project director during the design challenge. To maximize the potential for solutions, he gathered a cohort of 28 students from across the city to study the problem and design solutions as they saw fit. The teams met online with cohort leaders, using video conferencing software and digital presentation tools. Each team had a student facilitator that received special training, including how to gather resources, conduct online sessions, and build a successful team. Each cohort wrote problem definition statements that identified what they saw as the most pressing issue. For example, a common formulation was:

"Although young people would like to be more engaged with community service, many appear to be limited by a lack of transportation options."

Or:

"Although participating in the community is rewarding, a significant barrier to civic engagement is learning about what is going on."

After identifying the problem the cohort needed to solve, each group spent several sessions coming up with ideas that might address the challenge. Interestingly, most young people gravitated to the engaged citizenship model, which meant (for them) advocating for change and being active in the community. Several people spoke about their appreciation for military service and their connections to a large military base in the area.

Prototype and Test Scenarios

Each cohort then moved to the Prototype and Test phases of their design thinking project. The Prototype and Test phases involve creating a model of the proposed solution so that community members and stakeholders can interact with it and make improvements. *Prototypes* are not elaborate constructions but simple hand-held objects or visual depictions that allow team members to share their concept and get feedback on the proposed innovation. The goal of prototyping is to rapidly improve upon an idea, based on what team members and stakeholders can see, touch, or learn from.

Some common examples of prototypes are:

- A simple 3D model of your solution built with paper, tape, fabric, cardboard, or Lego
- A storyboard or picture book that narrates your idea in visual form
- A written document, such as a magazine article or branding story that imagines a future world impacted by your idea
- A mock book cover, album, or video game case, allowing people to visualize your solution as a commercial product
- A simple role-playing game or scripted narrative (such as a one-act play or imaginary transaction) demonstrating how your solution works
- Prototype software (or simple sheets of paper) that show how a user interface for your solution might look or operate

Each prototype is designed to rapidly solicit feedback from team members and community stakeholders about the content of your proposed solution. Since the prototype is a visual model of your concept, it is easy to make improvements on the fly by moving a few pieces of Lego, clay, cardboard, or other supplies. Remember that in rapid prototyping, feedback is the goal, not beauty or precision.

The goal of *testing* is to expose your solution to real-world conditions for a subset of your clients or customers. These scenarios allow you to see how actual users will like your solution—and what improvements they might suggest. (For example: Does your solution actually fix the problem that you have identified? If not, why?) Think of testing as a step closer to the actual implementation of your product or solution, just not at scale.

Testing may involve actual working models of software or technology, such as advertisements, websites, information systems, or data-driven systems connected to the cloud. In a social business, a test product might pilot an online learning system with potential customers, or experiment with a new strategy to welcome clients to a food bank. The key is that the design team has the opportunity to monitor the customer experience and collect data about what takes place during the initial implementation. Is it possible to measure the impact of your solution? What kind of measurement would be useful? Does the solution bring about the hoped-for change? Does it address the problem you defined during the second phase of design thinking?

Theory of Change and MVP

In Chapter 6, you'll learn more about testing your solution's assumptions by determining a *theory of change* statement for your innovation. This model will help you communicate to stakeholders why your solution will work and why people should invest resources in the idea. The Test phase actually begins this process, as you look for evidence about how effective your solution is for actual people. In design thinking, a test is a small-scale exercise in which you are gathering input in imaginary or staged circumstances. After that, you may choose to create a minimum viable product (MVP), which is an actual, working trial run based on your prototype and test experiences. An MVP is a bit like a "beta version" product or initiative in the real world. It usually incurs some expense, but it's generally less costly than rolling out a full solution to the marketplace (see Chapter 6). However, testing and MVPs still require some care, because how your product is perceived in the world matters. If your MVP is considered a flop, it will have negative consequences. For this reason, it is important to keep the Prototype, Test, and MVP phases separate. While it's perfectly acceptable to create numerous prototypes, you should only use the MVP process for solutions that appear to be desirable, feasible, and viable.

The civic engagement project Michael worked on provides a helpful example of what the Prototype and Test phases look like for a community-based social impact project. When the social innovation cohorts examined civic engagement barriers, they created lists of possible solutions, and advocated for them with local stakeholders, including administrators in Tacoma. To incentivize the group, a local foundation agreed to pay for an MVP that would test one of the proposed solutions in the coming year. The student teams each proposed a different prototype to encourage civic engagement among young people. Which of the following solutions do you think won the civic engagement contest?

1. **A Digital Event Calendar with Rich Data about Volunteer Opportunities.** The first team focused on the problem of

scheduling, realizing that young people have as much trouble as older people managing their schedules. Their prototype was a digital event calendar, which collected and presented all the civic engagement opportunities in the region. The team hoped that South Sound Together would update the calendar and create a smartphone app to connect to young people, sharing rich social media elements about volunteering.

2. **An Engagement Website that Matches Volunteers to Needs.** The second team approached the scheduling challenge in a different way. They proposed a civic engagement website that matched volunteers to community jobs and engagement opportunities. When young people sign in, the tool is populated with opportunities that match their user profile and local context. The team also envisioned a "digital rewards" system for attending events and completing tasks. Volunteer hours are tracked in this system and sent to local high schools or colleges.

3. **Civic Engagement Festival.** Moving away from web-based solutions, the third team recommended a civic engagement festival that brought community organizations together for a celebration and information fest. The event is hosted by a local organization with ample green space, such as a college or university. Moreover, a festival for young people featuring local bands and storytelling felt like a bigger draw than a new website. At the festival, there would be tables set up with volunteers recruiting for civic engagement opportunities, advocacy, and voter registration.

4. **Community Engagement Bus.** The fourth team proposed a community bus initiative that transports young people who want to learn about their communities directly to places where this work is being done. The bus would be painted by volunteer artists, and it would serve as a movable billboard for civic engagement activities. The community bus initiative could also be sponsored by local businesses that support in-service projects. A post Covid-19 solution, the community bus brings people together for a meaningful face-to-face experience.

5. **A Digital Enhancement to the South Sound Proud Website.** The fifth team proposed a digital extension to an existing community website. Rather than create something expensive and new, they reasoned that the infrastructure already existed for a retooled information hub that emphasizes civic engagement for young people. The new content would be written and curated by young people and civic engagement fellows, sponsored by local colleges and businesses.

After an afternoon of pitch decks and conversation, the community organizers selected the third option (Civic Engagement Festival) as the contest winner, partially because a local college volunteered to host the event and use each team as a resource to boost citizenship activities. However, South Sound Together lavished praise on all the teams that proposed innovative solutions. They recognized that each approach was grounded in empathy and compassion for local youth that wanted to support their communities but had challenges doing so. Most of the solutions overlapped in some way, and each was a response to the data that had been gathered. The design process had energized the community, brought together different groups, and connected funding to social impact projects. Design thinking moved the process forward in a collaborative way, which allows students and community members to test their ideas, propose meaningful outcomes, and make iterative improvements along the way. Rather than a top-down approach to innovation, managed solely by the city's administrators, the design process allowed young people a say in their own future, and encouraged them to design solutions that reflected their values, hopes, and dreams.

In the next chapter, you'll learn how a clear theory of change can amplify innovative ideas and communicate them meaningfully with team members, early adopters, and potential funders. Formulating a theory of change will also help you consider what resources your project will use, how your project will grow, and how the results should be recorded. The result is social impact.

Notes

1 Three pioneering books that turned the IDEO philosophy into a movement are: Tim Brown, *Change by Design: How Design Thinking Transforms Organizations and Inspires Innovation* (New York: HarperCollins, 2009); Tom Kelley and David Kelley, *Creative Confidence: Unleashing the Creative Potential Within Us All* (New York: Currency, 2013); and Tom Kelley with Jonathan Littman, *The Art of Innovation: Lessons in Creativity from IDEO, America's Leading Design Firm* (New York: Currency, 2001). For these materials and additional inspiration, see https://ideo.com.

2 IDEO tends to emphasize human-centered design principles in its materials for global audiences. For example, they explore how to design a planting system in Ethiopia that can be pulled through a muddy field by a single person. This type of solution is deeply embedded in a specific culture and requires a design that is focused on people and their context, not checklists from a catalog or different country. For an introduction to these ideas, see IDEO, *The Field Guide to Human-Centered Design* (2015), 112. www.designkit.org/resources/1.html. Accessed December 5, 2023.

3   Brown, *Change by Design*, 4.

4   For a list, see Code.org 2021 Annual Report (February, 2022), https://code.org/files/code.org-annual-report-2021.pdf. Accessed December 5, 2023. More about the origins of Code.org can be found in Michael J. Halvorson, *Code Nation: Personal Computing and the Learn to Program Movement in America* (New York: ACM Books, 2020), 368–70.

5   Teresa Chahine, *Social Entrepreneurship: Building Impact Step by Step*, Second Edition (New York: Routledge, 2023), 68.

6   Tom Kelley and Jonathan Littman, *The Ten Faces of Innovation* (New York: Currency, 2005), 16–21.

7   Source: Top Ten College Skill List. Data compiled by the U.S. Bureau of Labor Statistics, *Forbes* magazine, and the National Association of Colleges & Employers (2020). Related data can be found at: www.plu.edu/innovation-studies/careers.

8   Amy C. Edmondson, *Teaming to Innovate* (San Francisco: Jossey-Bass, 2013), 1.

9   IDEO, *The Field Guide to Human-Centered Design* (2015), 22.

10 United Nations, "Bringing Data to Life: SDG Human Impact Stories from Across the Globe" (2022), 30. https://unstats.un.org/sdgs/report/2022/SDG2022_Flipbook_final.pdf.

11 See Jeanne Liedtka, Randy Salzman, and Daisy Azer, *Design Thinking for the Greater Good: Innovation in the Social Sector* (New York: Columbia University Press, 2017), 4.

12 IDEO, *Field Guide to Human-Centered Design*, 24.

6 Developing a Theory of Change

After you have designed a new social innovation, the next step is developing a clear theory of change to articulate the vision for change, define desired outcomes, and strategize the necessary steps to achieve them.

Developing a theory of change ensures that there is a clear focus on positive social impact for clients, stakeholders, and communities. The process will also help ensure your interventions don't waste resources, stuffing shelves in a lonely warehouse or taking up space on a neglected website. A solid theory of change focuses an organization on projects that have tangible benefits which can be measured and assessed. In functional terms, it is a game plan that indicates when users do "x," they will help people or the planet achieve "y." This formulaic progression will help you establish an evidence-based approach for achieving impact. A good theory of change articulates how a social innovation *saves something* (time, money, or resources) or *gains something* (independence, security, equity, food, access, peace of mind, and more).

Theory-of-change planning typically involves data collection. It is the *empirical basis* that tests assumptions and justifies a proposed social innovation.[1] But what type of data should be measured, and what sort of activities should be tracked? Although there are several options, probably the easiest way to get started is to review your company's *mission statement* and consider related actions that can be measured. Too often, we observe that organizations rely on people counting or tracking unrelated activities, rather than behaviors related to *impact*. This is sometimes detectible when an organization only reports the number of "events hosted," "organizations funded," or "donations received" in stakeholder reports. Instead, *outcomes* of organizational activities should also be tracked, and show a clear support for the intended impact, which will be measured much later. Your theory of change can help capture these with measurable data outputs at each juncture of your process, aligning a company's work with specific changes in the sector's *ecosystem*. Some organizations refer to these outputs

DOI: 10.4324/9781003465669-6

as their measurements of *success*. Others go further and develop a *theory of action*, which is the specific delivery model that enacts your theory of change.

In this chapter, we'll explore theory of change as an essential planning process and communication signpost for social impact organizations. We'll discuss how a theory of change is defined in public interest technology companies, and how it is viewed through the lens of an ecosystem map. We'll look at organizations that use theory-of-change concepts, including an educational technology (EdTech) company that partners with public school districts, as well as a national nonprofit that provides workforce solutions for older Americans.

We'll also introduce the Agile software development lifecycle, and discuss how Agile methods can be used to support design and assessment practices in social impact organizations. We'll discuss the advantages of a minimum viable product (MVP) model, as well as the benefits of *ikigai*, a Japanese philosophy promoting creativity and happiness in public life. Finally, we'll share the insights of Susan Koehler, a private sector technology marketer turned social innovator and sustainability evangelist. Susan's career shows how a theory-of-change approach to problem solving can also influence an individual's career path, including creative work promoting the United Nations Sustainable Development Goals (UN SDGs) for human and ecological flourishing.

What's Theory of Change?

The term "theory of change" is being used regularly in the social innovation field—so much so, unfortunately, that it has taken on the trappings of a buzzword. We think this is confusing and unnecessary. If you aren't clear on how to use evolving terminology, you'll be reluctant to apply the concepts. A similar problem is the word "convenings" in social impact circles, a term meant to soften the term "conference," by making it seem less formal and academic. Behind both terms, however, is everyday speech. The simple truth is that a theory of change is synonymous with a framework for *purpose*. It is a way for an organization to test their assumptions and clarify what the benefits are of a new intervention in the community. To begin with, a theory of change can be just a list of outcomes or a good paragraph. Over time, the theory of change can be a valuable resource for describing the intervention for employees, donors, stakeholders, and community members.

One organization that aligns their theory of change with purpose is PEAK Grantmaking, a philanthropic organization that publishes their theory of change prominently on the organization's website. It reads as follows:

Our Purpose (Theory of Change)

We believe in principled grantmaking practices that align funders and nonprofits as equal partners in advancing their respective missions and strategic objectives. Narrowing the power gap and ensuring that funders live their values through their grantmaking practices will result in positive change for the causes and solutions we seek to collectively advance.[2]

In essence, the theory of change is a cause-and-effect correlation to what the organization's approach is to making a difference and how that difference will be measured.

One charitable organization that advocates for standardizing the components of a theory of change is the Annie E. Casey Foundation.[3] Based in Baltimore, Maryland, Annie E. Casey is one of the largest private foundations in the U.S. with assets worth over $4.2 billion. They recommend defining social change initiatives using three key areas: impact, influence, and *leverage*, meaning how much investment other organizations will add to the innovation model. Annie E. Casey has published a series of reports with practical guidance, templates, and examples to help organizations develop a theory of change. These can be used by nonprofit organizations and tech for good companies, as well as a range of strategic planning activities, such as developing an effective career path. Through this process, you can map outcomes in a manner that is either linear or causal. The exercise will also help you recognize and document underlying assumptions.

To determine how and when to use a theory of change, we appreciate the wise words of Dr. Maoz Brown, Head of Research for the ESG Initiative at the Wharton School of Business at the University of Pennsylvania. In an article entitled "Unpacking the Theory of Change," Maoz admitted that the term is as popular as it is confusing. Some of the challenge seems to have arisen from the desire to learn more about *how* rather than just *whether* social innovation programs work.[4] Like Maoz, we agree that by gaining a deeper understanding of the mechanisms of change within an organization or ecosystem, you can more effectively implement interventions that create positive social impact.

Documenting a Theory of Change

A theory of change makes it clear how your proposed social innovation will address or solve community problems, and how your project will be evaluated objectively. It's also the empirical basis underlying any social intervention. Successful organizations use a clear theory of change to amplify their ideas and share them with team members, early adopters, and potential funders. Documenting your theory of change will also help you consider what resources your project will use, how your project will grow, and how the results should be recorded.

To start, you can consider questions such as "How will the world be different if I am successful?" and "What makes my approach unique?" Defining your theory of change really comes down to determining what specific problem you are going to solve and how, exactly, you are going to do it. As Shelly's 94-year-old grandfather Ed Weber would say, how will you "get 'er done"?

Before you do anything, you need to ensure that there is enough room for improvement and know exactly where the problem is. This requires honest assessment and likely outside validation, too. In short, your innovation should not just be a great idea that you came up with about how to improve something or build something new. Be sure you aren't blinded by your passion, creating a solution in search of a problem.

Sometimes, the process of discovery reveals existing solutions that simply haven't been implemented in your target area or that your team has not heard about. It might be that your energy and passion would be best served supporting an existing organization, increasing their ability to scale. Oftentimes, we see nonprofit organizations, social entrepreneurs, and technologists replicate an existing solution and then split market share, only to end up alone on an island of redundant products. Partnering for social innovation is a neglected topic, and one that we take up in Chapter 8, where we discuss the power of scaling for social impact.

Market Landscape Analysis

After you confirm you have a problem really worth solving, your next step should be to conduct a thorough *market landscape analysis*. A market landscape analysis will help you determine *who* the potential customers or clients are for your product, *what* their needs and characteristics are, as well as the competitive environment or *ecosystem* in your industry. You can accomplish this by looking at comprehensive tech directories, conducting online research, reviewing government reports, and contacting organizations that are operating in your sector. This research will help you answer the "how" questions about the way that specific interventions work in your theory of change. You will also have a chance to add some substance to your *elevator pitch* (or 30-second product proposal), giving you a sense of what features or attributes give you the most traction. From there, you can build a more comprehensive eco-system map, summarizing the real (or virtual) neighborhood that you are moving into. An ecosystem map allows you to answer questions that arrive from customers and supporters about your theory of change. It allows your organization to understand how potential clients will see your business.

When Shelly and her team at Giving Tech Labs set out to create a new model for social innovation with X4Impact (now Giving Compass Insights), their ecosystem map showed a pretty crowded neighborhood with lots of competition. Giving Tech Labs used a version of the map to highlight who their proposed product would compete with and what other solution providers were offering. Examining the crowded field, but also market gaps, helped them to fine-tune their offering and explain it to partners and supporters.

Creating a Minimum Viable Product

A market landscape analysis and ecosystem map will help you learn about your marketplace and the products and services that other companies are offering. To test your theory of change and help you learn more about product delivery, it is now important to create a minimum viable product (MVP) to further test your assumptions. An MVP is a term borrowed from Agile software development principles, an iterative approach to building tech-nical systems that arose in the 2000s, especially within the soft-ware development community. Agile development stresses starting simple and building momentum through rapid cycles of testing and collaboration. It is an excellent model for social impact innovation.

An MVP is a bare-bones process or product that allows you to test assumptions and get immediate feedback. It is basically the least embarrassing version of your innovation that you can get in the hands of real users, designed to test systems and gain valuable feedback from workers and customers. It might be a scaled-down fundraising process that introduces a new strategy for managing fundraising officers and donor gifts. Or it could be a new soft-ware product or service within a tech for good company, such as a simple website that markets a product or delivers value to a test market. Either way, a trial run allows you to "eat the elephant in pieces" so that you can think big but start small.

Some innovators, like Dusty Davidson, a serial entrepreneur from Nebraska, uses the term "Most Lovable Product" instead of MVP, as a way to celebrate the moment when a team gets their beloved "baby" out into the world. Whichever way you define it, the idea is to move beyond the prototype and test stages of design thinking, in which you internally test a product, to getting the product in the hands of actual people. The MVP process also allows you to consider how your organization will produce and evaluate the product, including gathering data. (For more about prototyping and testing, see Chapter 5.)

Shelly has a personal insight into this. As a person who has started multiple companies *and* given birth to two human beings, she feels like having a baby is a pretty good analogy to the MVP process. For some reason, the magical stages of human gestation have a similar timeline to developing and releasing many products. Over nine months, a mother cares for and nurtures a child, protecting it from the world and preparing for the day when it arrives. If a human mother can create new life in less than a year, shouldn't innovators be able to construct a product in the same amount of time? At Giving Tech Labs, Shelly's teams took up the challenge, moving through the Empathy, Define, Ideation, Prototype, and Test stages, designing an MVP, and spending the final months on go-to-market campaigns. After launch, they allocated another nine months to make the project financially sustainable. By starting small and making iterative changes, the team increased the likelihood that the project would succeed.

Just Enough; Just in Time

The MVP approach also allows for rapid learning and process improvement. It allows you to focus on getting your venture off the ground with just the resources needed to thrive, nothing more. MVPs require fewer resources than fully scaled products. You want to put in *just enough* time, but not so much that you miss the market window identified in your landscape analysis. This style of product development is called the *just in time* approach, because materials and labor arrive just when they are needed, but no sooner. You pursue opportunities at warp speed, limiting your time and financial investments, delivering products to the market just when they need them.

Is it possible to perfectly time your market entry? Unfortunately, no. Even the most experienced entrepreneurs and investors have made the mistake of being too early or too late to the market. Both issues are equally problematic. An ill-timed scenario means that you miss the opportunity for a product or service to thrive. Being too early means that the market isn't ready and your message will require significant resources for educating customers and persuading them about your solution. If you are too late to market, it's likely that there will be entrenched competitors, and you'll be fighting an uphill battle for market share. Most organizations will have adopted their products, and they won't want to discard one solution for another that is untried.

There is also a *political risk* within organizations when you pitch leaders on backing once-in-a-business-cycle initiatives that have high growth potential but are also very expensive. (These are often called "moonshots," recalling the successful Apollo moon landings of the 1960s and 1970s). Moonshots require good economic conditions, favorable market timing, and lots of resources. Most of the time, it's better to focus on timing and market conditions that you can control, including a unique *value proposition*, which will help you explain why your product is special and the unique benefits that it will provide customers.

Progress over Perfection

A theory of change can include beliefs about market timing and risk. It should also allow you to think iteratively about your goals while you test your product and move through important milestones. Keep in mind the mantra of "progress over perfection" as you define your social impact objectives and outcomes. In fact, we encourage you to build your MVPs with little in the way of complex technology, relying instead on improving communication and automating processes to make them cheaper and faster. As we emphasized in Chapter 3, there are many pre-existing tools and infrastructures that your team may be able to use for little or no cost. These include electrical systems, smartphones, websites, public transit, radio, roads, and services provided by the government, nonprofit organizations, and charitable foundations. Consider how existing systems can support your MVPs. Start by seeing where the gaps are in current products or procedures. Then determine how revised procedures might benefit your users by saving them time or money. Consider the social or environmental benefits of doing something in a new or improved way.

As discussed in Chapter 5, before you create a new software application or product, design a prototype and test product to ensure that you have translated all of the necessary steps in the customer journey from "encounter" to "outcome." Create a journey map that imagines a customer experience like it is an excursion on a physical map. If you return to this image as you refine your theory of change, team members and stakeholders can suggest ways to simply or improve the process.

In addition, you can track or monitor a customer journey using off-the-shelf tools, such as Google Sheets or Google Docs. Use these applications for collating market research, surveys, interviews, and the feedback from focus groups. Modify the procedures in your MVP, determining the best way to deliver value to customers. Finally, test your marketing message and build rapport with your target audience. Connecting deeply with customers and clients is an important process that is often neglected by entrepreneurs rushing to market with promising solutions.

Technology for the Public Interest

Are there best practices for evaluating a theory of change and improving it? One strategy is to assess your approach by applying the principles of technology for the public interest (Tech4PI). Tech4PI is dedicated to leveraging appropriate technology and sustainable models to support social sector organizations delivering on their missions. The principles were developed based on experience creating and commercializing tech for good initiatives over many years. Inspired by the public interest law movement, Tech4PI has a common ethos.

Shelly and her team helped to establish these principles while working to define the best practices for problem solving in social impact settings. They developed their recommendations while creating solutions for immigrants and refugees, low-income students, the survivors of child abuse, early childhood education, impact-driven philanthropy, and more. The Tech4PI movement has also benefited from input by a seasoned advisory council, including representatives from leading software companies, philanthropies, nonprofits, social enterprises, and other experts. They learned from data captured over time, and solidified their principles as *guidelines* for successful tech for good companies. The following section describes these principles.

Principles of Tech4PI

- Build Long-lasting Operational Capacity with Sustainability Models in Place

  Tech4PI focuses on capacity building, resisting the temptation to use volunteers to build temporary solutions that are soon abandoned. Capacity building means helping to teach people to fish instead of giving them fish, because technology does not solve problems—people do. By focusing on systemic issues, Tech4PI can define sustainability models anchored on delivering value by saving costs, increasing capacity, achieving profitability through revenues, and attracting sponsors that are motivated by success measures.

- Measure Impact at a Systemic Level

  Tech4PI focuses on an explicit definition of measurable impact on mission delivery, with clearly defined key performance indicators (KPIs). It embeds the measurement of KPIs into the technology being offered, uniting the business model to the achievement of specific goals. Tech4PI aims to create technology and business models that deliver measurable, sustainable, long-lasting impact to improve people's lives by addressing a particularly urgent need, as defined by one of the UN SDGs or a related framework.

- Data Driven, Under Ethical Principles

  Tech4PI seeks to transform data into knowledge, working under ethical and privacy principles to process the data collected as part of mission delivery. This knowledge can help to reduce operating costs, increase capacity, identify opportunity areas, and accelerate learning by having access to data at a large scale. Most of us have experienced the negative effects of technology in some form, such as cyberbullying or the spread of misinformation on social media. This technology has been turned into a weapon by disseminating harmful content and selling users' data in the name of profit. Tech4PI tries to redress the balance by insisting on the ethical use of data and privacy principles.

- Centered on Empathy and Inclusion

  Tech4PI should create empathy and compassion, making us feel that we belong, are able to connect with others, and can collaborate, participate, and flourish as human beings. Although we have achieved some measure of progress through technology, many systems still distort social values and threaten the health of users by upholding negative values or stereotypes. For example, social media systems tend to exclude community members and advertise standards of beauty, success, or performance that are impossible to meet.

- **Change Through Collective Impact**

  To deliver systemic change requires the participation of society's different sectors. Tech4PI operates and thrives in an ecosystem where technologists can connect with and support organizations that serve the community and public interests. This includes nonprofit organizations, government, philanthropists, universities, and private sector companies operating under a crisp definition of impact with measurable improvement in human life and conditions.

Find Your Ikigai

Focusing deeply on community needs requires a mental attitude that is formed and shaped by values. We have often written about values in this book, and the importance of creating a mission statement that defines shared values and a sense of purpose for an organization. When social impact employees have a clear sense of "Why," it can serve as a guide to decision making and establishing a powerful theory of change.

Many people derive their values from their parents or extended family. Others are heavily influenced by community values or the principles of an organized religion. In the world of business, research shows that if your personal and professional values are in alignment, it can lead to greater productivity and a sense of fulfillment in one's work.

A useful way of expressing this balance is the Japanese concept of *ikigai*, a term that can be roughly translated as "your reason for being." There are many ways to apply ikigai, and a person's core values may change over time. But the concept is meant to be practical and motivational. Ikigai is your reason for waking up in the morning and getting out of bed.

If you search for ikigai online, you will typically find a collection of images representing ikigai as a Venn diagram asking these four questions:

1. What am I good at?
2. What do I love to do?
3. How can I make money?
4. What does the world need?

Each question might not apply to you. For example, many people who volunteer in social impact organizations are retired or not

Figure 6.1 Ikigai is a Japanese concept meant to restore balance in life, including personal and professional goals. The Venn diagram is designed to help individuals and organizations find what they are good at and what the world needs.

motivated by money. But it can be helpful to connect the concept of ikigai to the world of work. As you do so, you may begin to discover more about your ideal career path or vocation, including who you are meant to serve. Figure 6.1 invites you into this discovery process.

Sam Ushio, founder of the world's first cross-cultural event dedicated to ikigai, champions the use of ikigai as a scientifically proven method for improving longevity, creativity, productivity, and happiness.[5] He contends that ikigai isn't linked to financial compensation, rather living in harmony and having a life of purpose, lived intentionally. However, he acknowledges that work plays a significant role in many people's lives, and achieving ikigai may involve aligning one's career with a deeper sense of purpose. This is a good reminder that even those who aspire to change the world through their work will likely benefit from a holistic perspective on personal fulfillment.

We share the ikigai diagram to point out that technology should be oriented around what the world needs and what a specific organization is good at (or skilled in producing). Teams that identify a shared passion and can align their passion with true needs in the marketplace will do well personally and professionally. Tech4PI was designed to find and utilize this sort of balance, and the concept can be applied to most social innovation projects. There are many ways to apply ikigai in institutions, and it is worth taking the time to reflect on your journey from time to time. At the core of purpose-driven work is the recognition that each of us has something to do to support the communities we live in.

Equal Opportunity Schools

We've all heard the phrase "If it ain't broke, don't fix it." The problem is that we have lots of broken systems, whether we realize it or not. And the opposite is also true—we have many solutions in search of a problem, as evidenced by the $2.8 trillion social impact economy in the U.S., with increasing disparities in almost every social impact category. With over three million nonprofit organizations in the country, you would think that Americans would begin to consider consolidation or partnerships, rather than going it alone. However, it appears to be human nature to forge our own path. It's likely also part of our capitalist legacy, particularly in the private sector. The cycles of innovation, growth, and stagnation seem to motivate individual entrepreneurs to go it alone as they seek success.

While we encourage each organization to be creative and find new sources of value, it is encouraging to discover organizations that thrive by partnering with others. One such nonprofit is Seattle-based Equal Opportunity Schools (EOS), an organization that features educational technology as part of their theory of change. The following section presents the case for change developed by this social innovator.

A Focus on Success and Belonging

EOS is a nonprofit organization created in 2010 with the vision of identifying and supporting students that are underserved and underrepresented, especially Black and Hispanic students in high school. The goal was to support these students from initial recruitment into school through the completion of advanced placement (AP) courses and graduation. The EOS way focuses on building belonging and student success on a pathway to college readiness.

This includes future career planning through data, insights, and partnership development, working with local schools to put students at the center.

EOS focuses on creating interventions to prevent underserved and underrepresented students from missing out on access and opportunity in advanced courses and dual enrollment programs, where college credit is earned during high school. The organization works to reduce and eliminate opportunity and achievement gaps in AP classes. To date, they have created over two million student insight cards which reveal important information about untapped student potential. This is information not captured in GPAs and test scores alone. In fact, instead of those measures of success, EOS captures 43 data points using student diagnostic tools.

The new approach encourages underserved students to be seen, understood, and given resources. The interventions lead to better outcomes, including an additional 70,000 students enrolled in AP courses in 35 states across the U.S. Not only are there more diverse students enrolled in AP classes, but eight out of ten schools report that they maintain or increase the average course completion rates.

EOS is using a very specific theory of change to address what they see as an *opportunity gap*, an unequal distribution of resources and opportunities. The organization also looks at the *achievement gap*, the inequitable distribution of educational results and benefits. The organization's theory of change is based on the following assumptions:

- Equal access leads to unbounded human potential.
- Invitations to rigorous courses by trusted adults leads to greater sense of belonging.
- Academic intensity of high school curriculum leads to greater opportunity for positive post-secondary outcomes.

After over a decade of testing their theory of change, the organization adapted key elements of their approach and retooled their mission to broaden their impact from individual students to the educational system. This became the baseline of their *theory of action*, which is defined as the delivery model that enacts their theory of change. The EOS theory of action organizes program beneficiaries into three categories:

- Students
- Educators
- Schools, Districts, and States

Each beneficiary is supported by data-gathering methods that facilitate transformative learning experiences, as shown in Figure 6.2. The theory of action further suggests that some practices and policies need to be redesigned to be more effective for the program beneficiaries. Educators are encouraged to shift their mindsets from earlier training about student success and faculty responsibilities. Districts are also encouraged to review and improve their policies, which often serve as roadblocks for success.

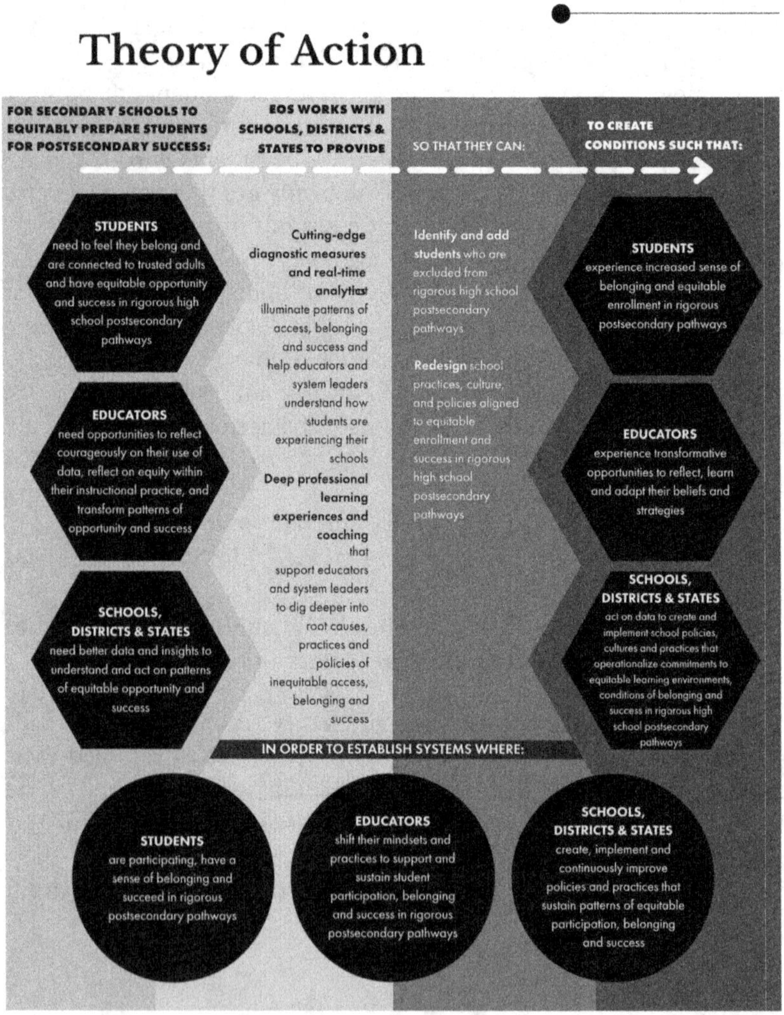

Theory of Action

Figure 6.2 The Equal Opportunity Schools theory of action, a plan that helps to deliver and enact their theory of change.

Secret Sauce

A theory of change helps an organization explain their secret sauce and how it will make a difference in the community by doing things their way. While theories of change have been used in nonprofit boardrooms for decades, you also have the opportunity to create a personal theory of change. It allows you to clarify your thinking about what you do in the world and why you do it. Much like defining a Why for individual action, a personal theory of change allows you to articulate your personal beliefs about why you act in the world and what sort of impact you think you will make. You can replicate an existing theory of change or create your own. The important thing is that you develop a plan for where you are headed and why you do the things you do.

Many people have similar vocational goals, but not all people get the same results. While there are many ways to accomplish a goal, there are also many ways to get there. No matter which route you take in your career, the most important predictor of success is having a plan that will work for you. This is especially important if you plan to accomplish social impact.

Agent of Change: Susan Koehler

Susan Koehler of Chandler, Arizona, is a great example of a social impact leader who has a personal theory of change. Susan spent her early years at Microsoft where she enjoyed a tenure of over ten years performing various marketing and operational roles. She went on to become the first Chief Marketing Officer at Rover.com, a Seattle-based startup that became a $1 billion publicly traded company focused on matching dog walkers with pet owners. (Similar to the online dating application, Bumble.) In 2024, Blackstone purchased Rover for $2.3 billion.

After spending time in corporate jobs and then a fast-growing startup, Susan started to think about her values and how they might align with the world's most pressing needs. She started to explore sustainability issues, and planned to live her values more authentically through her work. This path led her to work at environmentally focused companies, from material science to carbon emissions tracking. She realized that her true passion was working towards a vision of eliminating single-use plastics as a cause, and attempting to achieve environmental sustainability at scale. Her theory of change went through a cycle like the one shown in Figure 6.3.

As one of 48,000 members of the Microsoft Alumni Network, Susan joined Michael on stage at the first annual Microsoft

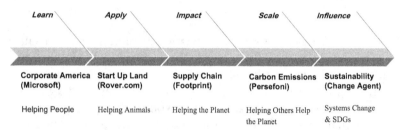

Figure 6.3 A personal theory-of-change model for Susan Koehler.

Connect Alumni Summit, which took place in September 2023, on the Microsoft campus in Redmond, Washington. The session was called "Maximizing Social Impact and Investing," where Michael and Susan were joined by Frank McCosker, a global finance expert driving social impact investments in Africa. They discussed creative business solutions that maximize impact and support the UN SDGs. The purpose of the session was to help the audience learn about large-scale investment opportunities, global development strategies, and upskilling for impact in higher education.

To the audience of former Microsoft employees, Susan shared her top ten trends in sustainable impact, which each represent a piece of her current work as a sustainability advisor, investor, and influencer. Her comments addressed everything from Formula E (international car racing with electric vehicles), to NEOM, a car-free futuristic Saudi Arabian smart city committed to 100 percent clean energy.

Whether or not you start with a large, audacious goal like sustainable packaging, or a small personal desire to make an impact in your community, a theory of change can be an important asset in your toolbox. It will also force you to articulate why you want to do something and how you will accomplish it. Thinking of your life as a process will allow you to see potential through-lines in your career and personal development. To learn more about how Susan Koehler applied her skills to curbing the use of single-use plastics in sports stadiums, see Chapter 8.

The Center for Workforce Inclusion

A theory of change is essentially a tool for strategic planning and keeping an organization accountable to its mission and purpose. But it's inaccurate to say that every social impact organization needs a detailed theory that explains how and why its programs work.

Allow us to introduce you to an innovative nonprofit organization that has been successfully operating for over 60 years. The

Center for Workforce Inclusion is a national nonprofit organization based in Silver Springs, Maryland, founded in 1962. They are one of America's oldest and largest nonprofits delivering employment programs to traditionally underserved job seekers, including Americans over the age of 50. They are funded through a federal grant program called the Senior Community Service Employment Program (SCSEP), which provides upskilling, reskilling, and job training to nearly 40,000 older adults each year in rural communities and urban centers throughout the U.S.[6]

The organization's visionary CEO, Gary Officer, started meeting with Shelly in 2019. Shelly and Luis Salazar were the keynote speakers at a global, nonprofit conference called Imagine: A Better World.[7] The conference was attended by hundreds of nonprofit and social impact leaders from around the world. At the time, Gary's organization was called Senior Services America. Gary recognized that, over the years, our increased lifespan and the nation's collective social context provided an opportunity to retool. Recognizing the outdated language of referring to people over 50 as "senior citizens," Gary and his team, including Chief Marketing Officer Rita Santelli, sought to modernize the organization's brand. This would give them an opportunity to expand their messaging and evolve the organization to address new opportunities in the private sector. The process led to the creation of a sister organization, run by Gary, as an independent, nonprofit tackling barriers to workforce equity.

Shelly and her team helped Gary, Rita, and their executive team embark on their new chapter. They rebranded from Senior Services of America, as they had been known for 60 years, to the Center for Workforce Inclusion (CWI). In name and focus, the organization broadened its reach. The CWI now runs a federally funded program to deliver job training, educational assistance, and support to low-income, older workers as they pursue meaningful economic opportunities. CWI Labs is a hub for cross-sector thought leadership focused on three key outcomes:

- Creating solutions driving equity through system change
- Educating policymakers by providing analysis informed through data
- Connecting with subject matter experts for new research and elevated content

Following the rebranding work, Shelly and her team engaged in an exploratory research project using artificial intelligence, a topic we'll return to in Chapter 9. Another example of this work is the Equity Summit, hosted by CWI, CWI Labs, and the American Workforce Coalition. The American Workforce Coalition is an initiative created by CWI Labs to bring fellow workforce development nonprofits together.

When asked about a formal theory of change, Gary admitted that his organization has no formal, written model explaining how their programs work. Instead, they have been fueled by a dynamic period of innovation and partnership, where the needs of their clients have taken center stage. Instead of a theory of change, Gary offered a compelling list of priorities:

- Our work is supported by a worldview that older workers require workforce opportunities, within a culture which values their worth.
- We believe in a world where nobody is excluded and where workforce investment dollars are equitably distributed.
- We believe in a world where change can only occur through inter- and intra-sectoral collaboration.
- We believe in a world where every single person, regardless of age, race, or gender, has an equal and respected place within the great aspirational mosaic, the United States.
- At our core, we are disruptive. We are crusaders for the aging and the marginalized. We believe this country can do better. Our new strategic plan will provide the roadmap for our journey into the future.

In our opinion, this list of values and priorities is more than sufficient. Although it does not contain all the elements of a theory of change, it reflects an intense focus on customers, clients, and communities. This is the core of social impact work.

Lessons from History

According to the Center for Theory of Change, Carol Weiss popularized the term "theory of change" as a way to describe the set of assumptions that explain both the iterative steps that lead to a long-term goal, and the connections between program activities and outcomes that occur at each step of the way.[8] Weiss challenged the designers of complex, community-based initiatives to be specific about the ideas guiding their work, and suggested that doing so would improve their overall evaluation strategies and strengthen their ability to claim credit for outcomes that were predicted. She called for an approach that seemed like common sense. Lay out the outcomes that are expected to occur as the result of an intervention, then plan an evaluation strategy around how the outcomes are actually produced.

This sounds pretty basic, right? Well, yes and no.

Like humans, organizations need to evolve and adapt over time. There is a famous meme that circulates on the Internet every few years. It says, "Evolve or Die," with a picture of a Blockbuster store with a dinosaur out front. Blockbuster was a ubiquitous video rental chain back when the prevailing entertainment media were VHS tapes and DVDs. Blockbuster was eventually put out of business when Netflix gained traction, and consumers became fed-up with late fees for keeping tapes and DVDs out too long. Blockbuster could have benefited from a revised theory of change—and probably a little more focus on customers along the way. A good theory of change can help social impact organizations from falling into the same trap.

In the next chapter, we'll look more deeply at how data is used in social impact organizations. We discuss creative ways to define success metrics, as well as how data collection and analysis will help you to be more effective in your initiatives and campaigns. Organizations that carefully record, analyze, and share rich data about their initiatives will receive innumerable benefits, including the ability to measure incremental progress, learn rapidly, adapt to change, and test assumptions.

Notes

1 See Paul Brest, "The Power of Theories of Change," *Stanford Social Innovation Review*, vol. 8, no. 2 (2010): 46–51, here at 49. https://doi.org/10.48558/N0V8-KR42. Accessed December 9, 2023.
2 For PEAK's current theory of change, see www.peakgrantmaking.org/about-us. Accessed December 9, 2023.
3 The Annie E. Casey Foundation, "Developing a Theory of Change: Practical Theory of Change Guidance, Templates and Examples" (Baltimore, MD: The Annie E. Casey Foundation, June 29, 2022). www.aecf.org/resources/theory-of-change. Accessed December 9, 2023.
4 Maoz Brown, "Unpacking the Theory of Change," *Stanford Social Innovation Review*, vol. 18, no. 4 (2020): 44–50, here at 46. https://doi.org/10.48558/N0V8-KR42. Accessed December 9, 2023.
5 Ushio is Chief Ikigai Officer of Connect3x Public Benefit Corporation. To learn more about his Ikigai projects, visit https://ikigailab.co. Accessed December 9, 2023.

6 For more information about this organization, see www.american-workforce.org.
7 For the conference recap and sessions, see https://aws.amazon.com/blogs/publicsector/imagine-a-better-world-a-global-nonprofit-conference-the-2019-recap. Accessed December 9, 2023.
8 For the quote and the organization's activities, see www.theoryofchange.org/what-is-theory-of-change/toc-background/toc-origins. Accessed December 9, 2023.

7 Data for Social Impact

This Little World explores how social impact leaders can use emerging technology and social innovation methods to create projects that are purpose-driven, scalable, and successful. Our content is centered on growth and leadership opportunities in the social impact sector, a global marketplace that brought in $2.8 trillion over the last year in the U.S.

To draw attention to the opportunities, we have highlighted Giving Compass Insights (formerly X4Impact), a data directory that presents information about thousands of organizations working to address social and environmental challenges. Using a common user interface and "dashboard," researchers can use Giving Compass to browse through thousands of solutions designed by and for people who are closest to the challenges. Rich data about trends over time, resource "deserts" (areas with limited access to services), and progress toward sustainable development goals (SDGs) are displayed visually with accompanying studies and reports.

Giving Compass Insights demonstrates how useful macro-level data is for organizations that are planning to innovate, invest, and partner with others. However, custom datasets can be just as useful *within* organizations, especially when they are investing resources, building new solutions, and tracking progress toward goals. In short, measuring and analyzing data is critical *both* to identify industry trends *and* to keep tabs on new social initiatives. When the data can be aggregated and shared, its value rises exponentially.

In Chapter 7, we take a comprehensive look at data measurement and how data is used in social impact organizations. We'll discuss creative ways to define *success metrics*, or quantifiable milestones that help stakeholders determine if a new strategy is working. We'll also introduce helpful reporting measures, including key performance indicators (KPIs), return on investment (ROI), and social return on investment (SROI). We'll discuss different data types, how data analysis leads to efficiency, and how common data models support organizations that want to collaborate with others. Data is omnipresent today; it is both a powerful tool and a potential liability

DOI: 10.4324/9781003465669-7

for businesses and consumers. For these reasons, we'll discuss how data security and privacy are just as important as data-gathering methods. Organizations that carefully record, analyze, and present rich data about their initiatives will receive innumerable benefits, including the ability to measure incremental progress, learn rapidly, adapt to change, and test assumptions. Using data well is also a prerequisite for *scaling*, or increasing the magnitude and impact of a social or environmental intervention that has proven its value.

Success Metrics and Innovation

In most social impact organizations, the overriding goal is to create positive change in society that can be measured and assessed. To do this work, it is important to record and analyze data, even if the ultimate goal is to solve a social or environmental problem that is hard to quantify using facts and figures. Simply put, the right data will persuade stakeholders and communities that your innovation is working, and it will help team members know that their efforts are gaining traction.

In a traditional business, gross revenue and profit are common baselines to measure how effective an organization is at fulfilling its mission. For example, a useful metric for evaluating profit is net margin, or the ratio of net profits to total revenues for a given time period. However, this type of financial data isn't the whole story for a social impact organization. Every nonprofit will carefully track assets, liabilities, and current income on a balance sheet. But its *success metrics* also include social benefits that are less tangible. These program "outputs" typically consist of clients served, services delivered, and other "indicators" that are related to social or environmental change. These impact metrics are often difficult to measure directly. For example, if an organization is attempting to reduce poverty or mitigate global warming, how will they know when they have "moved the needle" toward their goal? What measurable facts or milestones could be published in quarterly or annual reports that might demonstrate this? How can data alone demonstrate the effectiveness of a socially or environmentally beneficial program?

In Chapter 1, we introduced the tech for good company Forestmatic (www.forestmatic.com), a business founded to mitigate global warming by supporting the effort to sequester CO_2 gases in trees. Since trees are scientifically proven to capture harmful carbon dioxide and release oxygen, each new tree planted theoretically helps to clean the atmosphere. But what kind of data related to this initiative would be persuasive to potential users or customers? How granular should the data be, and how should it be presented? Since Forestmatic is a business-to-business (B2B) company, specializing in digital evidence related to tree-planting projects, they need to help their corporate customers gather data that can be passed along to clients and industry partners. They need to convince their stakeholders that beneficial tree-planting projects are taking place and can be verified. Forestmatic also needs to quantify carbon sequestration in a meaningful way, educating their clients without boring them with obscure facts and figures.

The company approached this challenge by creating tangible success metrics to share evidence about its environmental impact in real time. The company recognized that cloud computing and visualizer technologies had evolved to the point that it was possible to document global planting efforts visually, along with sophisticated mapping and verification data. Using a digital Tree Inspector (Figure 7.1), Forestmatic provides up-to-the-minute information about the journey a tree takes from planting to maturity. In other digital dashboards, the company displays the total number of trees planted, the megatons of carbon sequestered, and the total amount of forestland expanded by their partners' efforts. These progress indicators are success metrics, which they share with community partners, government agencies, and journalists who need to develop trust in the organization's business model and theory of change.

Social Return on Investment

Forestmatic also tracks internal data about its gross operating revenue (from selling its services to licensing partners) and gross profit (total income minus expenses) like any for-profit company. However, the company's *overall impact* is not measured simply by quarterly profit statements, but in relation to external success measures, such as progress toward shared sustainability goals, the number of new partnerships achieved, and the number of customers educated about carbon sequestration. This synergy between for-profit goals and overall impact is an essential business strategy for emerging tech for good organizations. The model balances financial return on investment (ROI) with a measure of social value for the planet called *social return on investment* (SROI).

SROI is important because it captures social benefit not indicated in financial statements. Highlighting SROI allows an organization to communicate the value of its work both internally (to employees) and externally (to clients and sustainability partners). When SROI

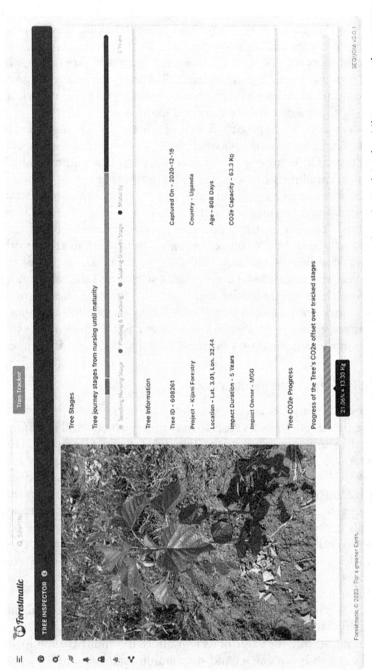

Figure 7.1 Forestmatic's digital dashboards, such as the Tree Inspector, show up-to-the-minute data about the company's success metrics.

is tangible and evident, ROI can come in lower than it might normally land in typical for-profit corporations. For example, an ROI that shows 3 percent to 5 percent profit is often adequate in a social impact organization if SROI is clear and tangible. In the tech sector, a popular strategy to generate positive cash flow and ROI is to use software-as-a-service (SaaS) as a revenue model. SaaS involves the sale (or subscription) of software services on the Internet, typically through a customer-facing website that charges for products or information. For more information about SaaS as a tech for good business strategy, see Chapter 3.

Quality data gathering makes it possible to prepare accurate ROI and SROI reporting for stakeholders. Tracking and analyzing corporate data is really an entire subfield of business management unto itself, with data-entry personnel, database specialists, data scientists, and machine-learning engineers collaborating to manage the data architecture of larger corporations. But small to medium-sized organizations can also benefit from data management best practices by focusing on a few key principles.

The first is recognizing the pitfall of *confirmation bias*, a snare awaiting social impact organizations that unconsciously look for evidence that their social innovation is solving a social or environmental problem, when it may not be.[1] For example, a homeless services agency may believe that the client services they are providing are reducing homelessness in a community, when the actual evidence about clients finding long-term housing is anecdotal and unrelated to the intervention that they have designed. (This can happen when data about a new intervention is not systematically gathered or tracked over time.) Success metrics can also be misleading when data gathering focuses on large, *cumulative numbers* (such as the number of "impressions" a social media post receives) rather than specific, targeted results, such as the amount of money spent to train a person who subsequently finds employment using the skills mastered.

Perhaps the most meaningless statistic of this type is the total amount of customers or clients "served" by an organization. The signage at McDonald's restaurants provides a humorous example of this phenomenon. Underneath the "golden arches" sign in front of many McDonald's is a statement that reads "Billions and Billions Served." While it has been estimated that McDonald's *has* served well over 300 billion hamburgers since its founding in 1955, the company no longer keeps accurate records of its total sandwich production globally. The "billions" number is a fanciful estimate, but the figure is almost entirely meaningless. A much more useful list of data-related questions might be: "Who regularly eats at McDonald's restaurants and what other things do customers do there?" "What is the average price of a meal at McDonalds?" "What are the most profitable items on the menu?" "How is the company's sustainability record changing over time?"[2] Many organizations fall into the "estimating" trap in their reporting, sharing information that is cumulative, but relatively meaningless. As a result, the data is not useful for SROI metrics or corporate reporting. In social impact organizations, we can and should do better with our interventions. Measuring data that is more granular and on-point can help.

What Data Should We Collect?

Although a deep dive into data analytics is beyond the scope of this chapter, the topic is closer to real life than you might imagine. Data is around us every day, and analyzing information is a core feature of the human experience. For example, it is a regular occurrence to hear work colleagues discuss how many *miles* they travel to and from work, how many *minutes* they exercise each week, and how many *days* it rains in their part of the country. (The answer for Seattle is 150 rain days per year, on average.) Beyond tracking personal data, however, many of us go farther when we use data for daily decisions. When thinking about the clothing you'll pack for a short trip, it's likely that you glanced at the weather report and predicted what the weather will be like where you are traveling. You may have also made your packing decision based on conversations with others and your individual assessment of weather data, past, present, and future.

In the workplace, data arises in many domains of an organization. Customer data about donors, employees, gift processing, and payroll is typically gathered and stored in a central database, protected from hackers and intruders. Financial data about wages, revenue, taxes, and other expenses is probably stored in a separate database system, and shared with the appropriate personnel. Customer and employee data is a treasure-trove of facts and figures that can help organizations see patterns, spot trends, and make informed business decisions. However, much of the information in corporations is not adequately structured, and it exists in systems that developed over time and are not fully compatible. Legacy systems hold data that was gathered using earlier protocols, with different formatting and organizing schemes. Moreover, when new initiatives or projects are started, the data is often gathered informally, employing whatever methods team members are familiar with.

The incompatibility of data systems is a problem for social impact organizations. It means that the data cannot be comprehensively used to generate business knowledge and insights without major effort. Data incompatibility is such an overriding concern that industry executives are writing full-length books on the subject, imploring corporations and consultants to take the issue seriously.[3] One of the most important reasons for this is that machine learning and AI tools rely on, to some extent, data that is well structured so that it can be verified, aggregated, and analyzed appropriately.

Data security is also important because most social impact organizations collect personal information about their clients. This data contains intimate information about people's lives, so organizations and technologists must collect, store, and use the data responsibly. According to public interest technologists Amy Sample Ward and Afua Bruce, this effort should begin with "minimizing the data collected in the first place: only what's needed for the project, and nothing more."[4] Building on this principle, organizations should consider who needs access to the data that is collected, and then restrict access so that no one inside or outside the organization can see or use sensitive information. This approach can reduce the chance of a data leak, which might be especially damaging for at-risk populations.

But what type of data should be collected to determine the effectiveness of a new product, service, or initiative? As noted above, success metrics are the meat-and-potatoes that will help you track the progress of a socially beneficial innovation. These are the data points that will help your organization fine-tune a social innovation and share excitement with others. In scientific language, success metrics are data that can be used to *validate or invalidate a hypothesis* you have created about an intervention you are planning.[5]

What does this data look like? Organizations that work to support customers or clients will have information that comes from a range of personal interactions, such as email, website sessions, social media engagement, purchase history, loyalty programs, and so on. The more customer data the better, as long as it is kept safe and secure in your database or customer relationship management (CRM) system. Rich data about customers and clients provides a "360-degree view" of relationships and interactions that enables faster and more accurate decision making for an organization. For example, in healthcare settings, rich diagnostic information about patients, combined with aggregated data about illness and treatment, is driving the rapid, low-cost, and accurate diagnosis of diseases in real time—a socially beneficial outcome enabled by data collection strategies and analysis.[6]

Although enterprise-grade CRMs like Blackbaud, Salesforce, and Microsoft Dynamics are getting the headlines in the social impact sector, it is surprising how effectual "low-tech" data-gathering tools can be for small to medium-sized organizations that are looking to gather data, measure progress, and refine their offerings. Data tracking is another place where we recommend that you "think big but start small" in your approach to data management tools and procedures. For example, if you are prototyping or testing a new social innovation, Microsoft Excel or Google Sheets will be more than adequate to store thousands of records and make them available to key team members. Ultimately, most data are simply rows and columns of information that can be used to track the progress of initiatives or behaviors over time. The key is selecting the right information or "indicators" to store, and agreeing on a standard way to store, analyze, and use the data. You don't need to save everything. As Teresa Chahine of Yale University writes, "The fewer indicators you deem sufficient to demonstrate success, the better."[7]

Case Study: An MVP that Measures Impact

A traditional guideline for data-gathering metrics is to make them SMART: specific, measurable, achievable, realistic, and time bound.[8] Intermediate metrics will help you track your progress along the way, and give you information that you can use to change course, as needed. At Pacific Lutheran University (PLU), Shelly and Michael spent six months recently with a team of social innovators who were interested in measuring the quantity and quality of social impact projects that the university had initiated over the past five years. Campus leaders were interested in expanding their social impact partnerships, but before doing so, they wanted to study just what the institution was doing in terms of social impact work. They sought answers to important questions, including "How many social impact projects has our institution designed, funded, or launched in the past five years?" "What organizations have we partnered with or served?" "What tangible results have we achieved?" What service gaps or opportunities does the aggregated data reveal?"

The initial goal was to build a minimum viable product (MVP) consisting of 300–500 database records that stored the following information:

- Documented community challenges seeking solutions
- Programming and initiatives within the university that addressed social and environmental challenges

PLU suspected that it was doing more in the community than interacting with others through its traditional academic programs. Although students in Nursing, Business, Social Work, and Education were regularly doing community-oriented service projects, so were staff and faculty in music, athletics, the performing arts, STEM, innovation studies, alumni initiatives, and diversity and inclusion programming. There were also student groups that were active, community-based learning centers, business development initiatives, community workshops, and annual events hosted on campus, such as the Special Olympics. The group also recognized that impact activities might be collated to the United Nations Sustainable Development Goals (UN SDGs), a framework that by 2022 had been used by about half of the nonprofit and for-profit organizations in the U.S. that described their work as social impact.

Our MVP was not an expensive, custom-designed application, but a simple "off-the-shelf" Google Sheets spreadsheet with rows and columns designed to store essential project information. Each row in the spreadsheet was a database *record*, with columns (or fields) that captured impact project data such as the community project name, originating group, project type, project short description, UN SDG category, expected reach (local, country, or global), funding status, contact data, and so on. A *data dictionary* contained a description of each field value and its expected data type, such as String, Date, Boolean, or URL.

The entire project was managed using one spreadsheet containing 500 rows of data. However, to simplify data input a Google *form* (or online questionnaire tool) was created by team members to allow for safe and accurate record insertion in the spreadsheet. (A custom form prevents incomplete or inaccurate records from being inserted into the collection, and allows for bespoke instructions and fillable input boxes and controls.) Collectively, this served as the software system for our project.

At PLU, a team of social innovation interns gathered information from across the university and inserted it into the spreadsheet via our tools and procedures, canvasing the organization for proposals, projects, grants, research agendas, events, and partnerships related to social impact. Importantly, our MVP was a "live" dataset, with summary information that was updated daily. A QR code allowed for easy access to the website and user-entry form. (See Figure 7.2 for the first team members and a laptop showing our website and QR code.)

Shelly and her team created a digital dashboard, so that a running total of projects and indicators was visible to team leaders. Michael

Figure 7.2 The Social Impact Project team at Pacific Lutheran University (Garfield 208 Cafe), March, 2022. Left to right: Felix Halvorson, Shelly Cano Kurtz, Michael Halvorson, Mary Campbell, and Heven Ambachew. (Photo credit: John Froschauer.)

created a public-facing website to encourage members of the community to insert their own records, which were received through the Google form and validated according to our data-entry scheme. The dashboard was prominently displayed on the organization's website, and it presented visual information about KPIs, including the total number of projects, the top-ten areas where social impact work was taking place, a snapshot of changes over time (reflecting a sense of momentum in the data), and the relevant UN SDG each business unit was addressing. Faculty, staff, students, alumni, and community members were able to use the information to plan new initiatives, events, and curricula. Importantly, the data we gathered allowed stakeholders to avoid duplicating efforts when they initiated a new project. If another initiative already existed in the ecosystem they were considering, workers could contact one another to collaborate, rather than rebuild an intervention that was already working. (See Chapter 8 for additional examples of collaboration and partnership, a critical component of scaling.)

We present our social impact project at PLU to offer a tangible example of how impact data can be collected and assessed through low-cost, off-the-shelf mechanisms. This MVP provided a five-year snapshot of social impact work in the organization, identifying previously unknown areas of innovation and entrepreneurship that were present in the community. KPIs such as the total count of social impact projects, locations for this work, statistics about the project type, and trends across time gave administrators the insights they needed to better evaluate and coordinate projects in the local impact ecosystem. It also allowed administrators to establish *targets* or quantifiable goals that allowed them to determine the right mix of projects to sponsor in the community.

One of the outcomes was a realization that the university did not have adequate record-keeping methods, because a lot of unrecognized business activity was discovered. The university's data architecture was robust, but focused on traditional teaching and learning outcomes rather than community engagement. This emphasis prioritized academic data inputs, such as earned credit hours, progress toward majors and minors, tuition revenue, recruiting data, and so on. However, the university had been a major innovator in community engagement and outreach, and that data was being lost.

The administration responded by creating a new office of institutional effectiveness, designed to build the infrastructure necessary to monitor and track a wider range of projects and data sources. They also established a Blue Zones Project Center on campus to coordinate community development activities. The university anticipates that over time its role as a community anchor will continue to grow, allowing the institution to function as a convener where the community's self-identified needs are discussed, coordinated, and delivered. This is an example of *collective impact* in which coordinated work in the community is accomplished by a range of organizations, including regional nonprofits, government entities, foundations, and voices for advocacy and care in the region. At the heart of this collective action will be the thoughtful use of data to assess social impact.

Exploring Common Data Models

As the previous case study demonstrates, rich institutional data can help an organization track progress and discover meaningful insights about a community and its assets. When a new innovation becomes part of an organization's regular portfolio, it is important to find a standard way of storing the data, so that it can be used by different teams in the corporation or community. This means using a common data model for information gathering and analysis. A *common data model* is a way of representing different types of information in an organization through labeling, formatting, and relationships that can be used across projects and applications. Traditionally, when you create a new data set and label its fields with terms like "patient_id" or "team_name," the labels in your application are specific to the project you are working on. The project's data is structured and labeled in a way that is specific to your new innovation and nothing else.

However, in larger organizations, there will be hundreds of data sets like the one you are building, as well as numerous data-centric applications and tools. If each project uses a different set of *schemas* (or protocols) to define its data, it won't be easy to combine or analyze the information collectively. To avoid this limitation, it is important for social impact organizations to use a common data model for data-gathering initiatives that are expected to grow and be shared across the organization. A common data model will also allow for data repositories to be aggregated and processed by AI tools and machine-learning systems.

In 2018, Microsoft introduced a paradigm called the *Microsoft Common Data Model for Nonprofits*. It is openly accessible and available for use with any data management system, including applications from other solution providers, such as Blackbaud or Salesforce. We highlight Microsoft's common data model here because it was specifically designed to support social impact organizations, whether they are defined as for profit, nonprofit, nongovernmental organization (NGO), or other entity. Microsoft's common data model also shares some of the same attributes and organizing principles as Microsoft Dynamics 365, a suite of interconnected applications designed to support many business needs, including resource planning and customer relations.

The Microsoft Common Data Model for Nonprofits system contains extensions to support a wide range of data-gathering activities that are typical for social impact groups. Rather than creating your own headers, labels, and relationships for storing information, we think it will be helpful for you to use a common data model to define them. When you share your information with others later, or feed your data into machine-learning scenarios, it will be easier to create structured or aggregate data sets and compare "apples to apples."

Some of the benefits of the Microsoft Common Data Model for Nonprofits include:[9]

- Standard definitions of terms that will be useful for data gathering in organizations, including contact management, fundraising, awards, program delivery, and impact tracking data. Over 90 data definitions and relationships are predefined, so you don't have to make them up.

- Templates that your organization's clients or partners can use to help data analysts create *logframes* (logical frameworks, the building blocks of effective program design).
- Terminology related to the UN SDGs, which you can deploy to standardize program measurement and outcome tracking.
- Lower costs for social impact organizations. When you use predesigned, industry-standard terms and scenarios, it takes less time and money to design data management systems.

Until now, we have been discussing how data can be stored and used *within* organizations to solve specific internal goals, such as managing customers, tracking new social impact projects, or supporting decision making. However, some organizations also find they want to share data externally, to support research or collaborative solutions in the community. In this case, they use a common data model so that they can create open data and data collaboration resources for the community. *Open data* is widely shared information that is put to work to solve socially or environmentally beneficial concerns, such as reducing poverty, addressing climate change, closing the broadband gap, or building skills for jobs. To do this work, leaders need to publicly discuss the data they have, advocate for collaboration, and ensure the quality and trustworthiness of their information. Leaders need to use a system for sharing information that is outward facing, such as the Open Data for Social Impact Framework, supported by the Open Data Institute (https://theodi.org) and other organizations.[10]

A model for this type of collaboration comes from the public health sector, where information about infectious diseases and other maladies is widely distributed by scientists and researchers. This involves the open sharing of scientific data that is searchable, accessible, and reusable, opening doors for research and innovation. The same sort of data sharing is now being encouraged in the social impact field, so organizations can collaborate on challenging problems, rather than working with just a subset of relevant information. Although the schemas of the Open Data for Social Impact Framework are beyond the scope of this chapter, the fact that it exists and is in active use demonstrates another reason why common data models are so important for organizations to consider.

Guardify's Data Management Strategy

In Chapter 3, we discussed how Guardify (formerly VidaNyx) used digital transformation to improve the way that child advocacy centers manage video evidence. In an effort to protect children, law enforcement agencies had followed a convoluted process to record, safeguard, and distribute video tapes containing sensitive material about children, including testimonies of abuse and neglect. Guardify came up with an innovative data management strategy to safeguard and distribute this sensitive material. When the new system became active, agencies were able to save up to 90 percent of the total cost per case. There is also a tenfold improvement in the way that child advocacy centers operate. Guardify's data management strategy is a successful social innovation. It frees up financial and human resources that can be used to serve more children, shifting the programmatic focus toward prevention and ending the cycle of abuse that up to 700,000 children experience annually in the U.S.

Since its founding in 2018, Guardify has been a success story for families and communities. However, with an issue that is so sensitive, how did they communicate the program's value to child advocacy centers and other stakeholders? The list of potential clients includes law enforcement agencies, advocacy centers, child protective services, district attorney's offices, government officials, and families. What information would convince these groups that Guardify has a product and data strategy worth investing in?

The solution in this case was rich data. Guardify strongly believes that the survivors of abuse deserve better industry practices to protect and preserve their private information. For this reason, they created a data management system that is protected through military-grade encryption technology. But they also recognized that accurate information about the time and costs savings produced by advanced technology would help their clients see the financial benefits of managing information in new ways. To make this point, they began to quantify time and financial savings through KPIs that show the savings quantitatively and visually.

The social innovation team at Guardify created a journey map to chart out each step of the existing video recording, safeguarding, and sharing process. They studied how long the existing process took, how many people were involved, and the labyrinthine process for requesting video testimony when existing VHS tapes were ordered from a law enforcement evidence "lock up" and driven to a regional district attorney's office. The group summarized the process and quantified the steps as "chain of custody actions," a standard measurement in the law enforcement field. They also measured details such as the time to produce accurate transcriptions of video tape evidence and the total amount of time law enforcement agents need to procure new interview evidence.

The Guardify team studied the journey map and looked for ways to improve the process of recording videos, safeguarding them, and distributing them. They proposed several technology improvements, including secure cloud computing via Amazon Web Services and a custom website that would allow authorized users to view evidence. Then, for each agency that adopted the practice, they tracked overall time savings related to evidence management, routing, and the total "person hours" saved. Using financial metrics, they were able to translate the time saved into dollars saved for agencies that adopted the Guardify platform. Finally, in marketing and sales materials, company representatives were able to share with potential customers the savings they might achieve by adopting the platform.

Digital Dashboards

Guardify's business proposition was twofold: they expected to increase the safety and security of access to sensitive material, and they expected to save agencies money when they adopted the platform. Overall sales and adoption metrics also demonstrate the momentum experienced within the industry due to the new social innovation. By the end of 2022, Guardify reported that 190,000 forensic evidence videos had been uploaded to their secure website, and the materials were routed 8.5 million times collectively to trusted partners. This represents a cost savings of up to 90 percent of the total cost per case, when comparing Guardify to the traditional method of video routing and storage. By late 2023, over 214,000 children have been served and protected by the data system, and the number increases dramatically with each new agency that adopts the software. More than 12,500 agencies across the U.S. are now Guardify customers. Law enforcement officers alone have saved over 139,000 hours procuring and tracking video evidence.

Figure 7.3 shows a digital dashboard with this information, which the company presents on its website to inspire customers and industry stakeholders. A digital dashboard is a graphical tool that allows users to spot top-level trends within the data quickly. It is typically updated daily or weekly with fresh information. We present one of Guardify's digital dashboards here to bring home the point that many tech for good companies are using live data to advertise and promote their products. The information is useful both to internal teams, so that they can track their progress toward goals, and to external groups, so that they can learn how effective this social innovation is.

Figure 7.3 Guardify displays its success metrics on a digital dashboard that users can access through the program's menu-driven interface. Visual representations of data can help users understand current goals and overall impact within a sector or industry.

In the book *Power to the Public: The Promise of Public Interest Technology*, authors Tara Dawson McGuinness and Hana Schank emphasize that current, up-to-the-minute data is the most effective method for an organization to advertise its social impact.[11] In the past, nonprofit organizations tended to publish quarterly newsletters or annual reports to share their triumphs and success stories. But today, real-time impact data is the norm, even for small to medium-sized organizations. We saw several examples of this in this chapter, including Forestmatic, Pacific Lutheran University, and Guardify. Each organization developed success metrics, gathered data, and used digital dashboards to display information for customers and stakeholders. If you embed data-gathering schemes into your social innovation projects, and use a common data model to share information, it will be straightforward for you to track, evaluate, and iteratively improve your projects. Think big, start small, and move from data to insight.

In the next chapter, you'll learn to use data to build scalable solutions in social impact organizations. We'll investigate several organizations that have increased the magnitude of their projects and interventions globally. We'll explore how to leverage your work with partnerships, rather than adding expensive headcount. You'll also learn to use digital methods to increase efficiency, fine-tune your theory of change, and develop innovative revenue models to make growth sustainable. Finally, you'll learn about the work of the Bill & Melinda Gates Foundation, which has used scaling principles to save lives and reduce suffering at a global level.

Notes

1   Ann Mei Chang, *Lean Impact: How to Innovate for Radically Greater Social Good* (New York: Wiley, 2019), 73.
2   To learn the answer to some of these questions, including the connection between McDonald's and the movement for civil rights in America, see Marcia Chatelain, *Franchise: The Golden Arches in Black America* (New York: Liveright Publishing, 2021).
3   Most recently, former Microsoft executive Bob Muglia; see *The Datapreneurs: The Promise of AI and the Creators Building Our Future* (New York: Peakpoint Press, 2023). Michael's recommendations about appropriate data architecture within organizations can be found in Michael Halvorson, *Microsoft Visual Basic 2013 Step by Step* (Sebastopol, CA: O'Reilly Media, 2013).
4   Amy Sample Ward and Afua Bruce, *The Tech that Comes Next: How Changemakers, Philanthropists, and Technologists Can Build an Equitable World* (New York: Wiley, 2022), 75–76.
5   Chang, *Lean Impact*, 76.

6 Data.org, "Workforce Wanted: Data Talent for Social Impact" (2022), 19. https://data.org/wp-content/uploads/2022/06/Workforce-Wanted-Data-Talent-for-Social-Impact.pdf. Accessed December 5, 2023.
7 Teresa Chahine, *Social Entrepreneurship: Building Impact Step by Step* (New York: Routledge, 2022), 130.
8 Chahine, *Social Entrepreneurship*, 118.
9 This list of benefits was current when the book went to press. For a current list of features, see https://learn.microsoft.com/en-us/dynamics365/industry/accelerators/nfp. Accessed December 5, 2023.
10 For a summary of the initiative, see https://news.microsoft.com/open-data-social-impact-framework. Accessed December 5, 2023.
11 Tara Dawson McGuinness and Hana Schank, *Power to the Public: The Promise of Public Interest Technology* (Princeton, NJ: Princeton University Press, 2021), 35–39.

8 Scaling for Impact

Your social impact project is showing signs of success: It produces tangible social benefits, addresses the needs of customers and communities, and is financially viable. What are the next steps for your social innovation? Should you be content with slow and steady growth? Or is there a way to rapidly increase the scale and social impact of your project? What resources and best practices would you need to consider to do so? Is there also a way to partner with others so that your solution becomes a positive force for change in society?

In Chapter 8, you'll learn to build capacity in social impact organizations to unlock the power of innovative projects, campaigns, and interventions. You'll learn how to *scale* innovations, meaning to increase the relative size and scope of a project so that it influences more people in more locations. You'll explore the essential business conditions required for scaling, based on resent research and our personal experience of scaling tech for good projects. You'll also learn to use digital methods to increase efficiency, fine-tune your theory of change, and develop innovative revenue models to make growth sustainable. To illustrate our recommendations, we share stories of impact from the Bill & Melinda Gates Foundation, Footprint, Giving Compass Insights, Google, Microsoft, the National Institutes of Health, and the YMCA.

What Is Scaling?

Throughout *This Little World*, we've encouraged social innovators to *think big but start small* in their approach to social entrepreneurship. In this chapter, we flip the script. We describe how you can take an existing project or intervention and grow it rapidly so that the innovation can serve more people better. At this point, we'll assume that you have a new social innovation, be it a product, service, or campaign, which has shown potential and is gathering data to establish its value to clients or customers. *Scaling* means to increase the magnitude and reach of this project so that it can have

DOI: 10.4324/9781003465669-8

a deeper, more sustained impact on real-world communities. From an organizational point of view, scaling allows a business or nonprofit organization to do more of what it is good at, extending its reach into new domains and contexts.

In *Innovation and Scaling for Impact*, Christian Seelos and Johanna Mair provide a helpful description of the innovation process. They distinguish the creative act of *innovation* from the strategic business activity of *scaling*. Seelos and Mair write, "Innovation generates the potential for impact creation. Scaling creates impact from innovation."[1] This means that the creative process of designing and testing a new product is different from the decision making needed to launch and scale a new product in the marketplace. The business decisions related to scaling are dependent on a number of external factors, including evaluating organizational resources, sizing up competition, selecting a revenue model, considering economic conditions, and fine-tuning for operational efficiency. Each of these factors will have an influence on how the organization moves from linear, iterative growth to exponential growth, or growth at scale.

Bill Drayton, the founder of Ashoka and one of the pioneers of social entrepreneurship, has written that broadly delivering innovation at scale is at the heart of the social entrepreneurial mindset. Modifying a popular analogy about "teaching a person to fish," Drayton writes:

> Social entrepreneurs are not content just to give a fish or to teach how to fish. They will not rest until they have revolutionized the fishing industry. Identifying and solving large-scale social problems requires social entrepreneurs because only entrepreneurs have the committed vision and inexhaustible determination to persist until they have transformed an entire system.[2]

Social entrepreneurs are not just moved to launch a product or improve a process. They want to change the world in meaningful ways and contribute to human and ecological flourishing. Social innovation at scale allows entrepreneurs to address what they see as the world's most vexing social and environmental problems. Their overriding goal—deep social impact—is a comprehensive task that requires ingenuity, leadership, strategic planning, inclusive practices, partnerships, and more.

A helpful term in the discussion about scaling is *replication*. If a social impact organization has a new product or intervention that is successful, what is the best way to replicate that success in other settings or contexts? Replication in a nonprofit ecosystem is a little like opening a new "franchise" in the world of business. It takes an innovative product or service and transfers the concept to dozens (or hundreds) of other areas. As Jeffrey Bradach has written:

> At the heart of replication is the movement of an organization's theory of change to a new location. In some cases, this might entail transferring a handful of practices from one site to another; in others, the wholesale cloning of the organization's culture.[3]

The benefit of the replication model for scaling is that it allows a service organization to grow by creating partner franchises that draw resources from a shared network or central office. While many social entrepreneurs are reluctant to give up direct control of their initiatives, this strategy can be a powerful way to seed transformative change across an entire industry. To achieve scale, the core objective of a social impact organization must be to solve a vexing social problem, rather than maintain personal control over the specific implementation of a solution.[4]

Scaling allows an organization to share immediate and predictable benefits with new communities, and to increase the depth and reach of those benefits. Typically, the benefits of scaling extend to more than one product or service—it results in a continuous stream of improvements throughout a sector or marketplace, expanding current activities, products, and services.[5] Historically, this has led to massive changes across society, especially during the technology surge of the late nineteenth and early twentieth centuries. At this time, the benefits of technological innovation led to major enhancements in the communication, transportation, power, and healthcare sectors of the economy, so that millions of people benefited from new discoveries in science, business, and medicine.

Scaling has also led to impressive results in the social impact sector, bringing major social and environmental benefits to society. Recent examples include the expansion of humanitarian organizations such as Habitat for Humanity, the Red Cross, and the United Way. An example of tech for good scaling is the recent effort to distribute broadband Internet technologies to underserved communities in the U.S and around the world. This has been a multi-organization initiative over the last few years leveraging private philanthropy, government organizations, and tech innovators like Broadband Telecom and WiFi to the Rescue. These organizations started with a framework like UN SDG #11: Sustainable Cities and Communities, developed a theory of change, focused on economies of scale, exploited low-cost infrastructures, and built "last mile" capacity to deliver broadband connectivity to cities, rural areas, and neighborhoods. The initiative prioritizes economic growth and delivers measurable social return on investment (SROI), contributing in tangible ways to the well-being of millions of people.

The 80/20 Rule

If scaling implies a rapid expansion of pathways for your social innovation, how should an organization think about the features of their products and the true needs of clients and customers? Is it possible to scale products so that they satisfy the needs of *all* potential adopters? Or should an organization divide its market into *segments*, organized by customers that share common characteristics? In this section, we discuss creative ways to think about the clients or users for your product, focusing on their core needs and wants, which should correspond closely to the features of your product.

As you learn about scaling, a rule of thumb from behavioral studies might help. The 80/20 rule in business, also called the Pareto Principle, suggests that 80 percent of your results will come from 20 percent of your effort. This guideline implies that organizations need to spend their time focusing on what is most important for their customers and products—that is, the features and strategies that will attract the largest, most motivated group of people. Rather than designing an expensive, comprehensive product that satisfies *all* the needs and desires of consumers, it is best to lower the overall cost of the product and focus on 80 percent of what consumer groups really need. The underlying principle is that, at scale, it is virtually impossible to satisfy the needs of *all* customers with a product. For one thing, some customers will value simplicity and minimalism, while others will value comprehensive systems.

The 80/20 rule is essentially a guideline to remind teams that they should think about the core features and benefits an organization provides. Which features are absolutely required to satisfy your theory of change? Which qualities or elements raise costs and are ultimately used by just a small subset of people? Can you create something that is both smaller and better? Is there a mix of features that would appeal to 80 percent of your customers?

We first learned about this principle through our work in the software industry. During our conversations with Microsoft and its industry partners, we discovered that high-end computer users were always on the lookout for cutting-edge productivity features in their software products, such as the data analysis tools in

Microsoft Excel. During the 1990s and early 2000s, the product development teams at Microsoft were highly skilled, and they regularly provided impressive new features in their core products. However, these features were used by a smaller and smaller percentage of users over time. Paradoxically, the most sophisticated features served to *limit* the market for products like Microsoft Excel and Microsoft Word. The advanced capabilities made the products more expensive to purchase and harder to use. However, many of the key decision makers in corporations loved them.

In the 2010s, Google developed a portfolio of modest business applications that could be launched online and run through a web browser. Google distributed these online tools for free, selling upgrades to the core products if users wanted more advanced features. At first, industry pundits criticized Google Apps because the productivity tools were so bare-bones. But over time, many customers realized that Google Docs, Google Sheets, and Google Slides could do about 80 percent of what most people did in Microsoft Office—and for a much lower cost. Google Apps (later Google Workspace) was particularly attractive to nonprofit organizations and educational institutions, which were always short on funds and preferred to acquire simplified tools that could be used across their organizations. Rather than selling a comprehensive application suite that satisfied *all* the wants and needs of a range of customers, Google satisfied *most* of the wants and needs of typical users, offering their product as an extra convenience for customers that also adopted Gmail, Google Drive, and other Google products. Microsoft was forced to redesign its Office suite as Microsoft 365 (a Web-hosted product) and lower the cost of its entry-level releases to compete. According to Statista.com, Google's office suite controlled over 50 percent of the market worldwide in early 2023, displacing Microsoft as the industry leader.

The 80/20 rule is not a mathematical formula, but a guideline designed to help organizations focus on the core features and attributes that will achieve the best results for a large group of customers. This does not mean that organizations should neglect underrepresented groups or diverse audiences. Rather, it means that highly scalable products should address common needs and aspirations first. It can be tempting to design boutique products for unique customers, but in doing so, you will likely be ignoring the financial needs of many potential clients. Determine what is most useful and bring that to scale, setting aside elements that likely have little to do with success.[6]

Disruptive Innovation

The Google Apps case study is an example of *disruptive innovation*, when a relative newcomer to the market disrupts a market leader by satisfying the core needs of neglected users, dramatically lowering the price while still providing suitable functionality. Disruptive innovators do not simply shake up an industry or improve existing products; they appeal to low-end, underserved customers, who gratefully adopt their products. Disruptors then attempt to migrate "upmarket" to the mainstream with their offerings. By the time industry leaders notice the new rival, it may be too late to stop them.

The late Clayton Christensen popularized the concept of disruptive innovation in a book entitled *The Innovator's Dilemma*.[7] In a recent *Harvard Business Review* article, Christensen and his co-authors reflect on the theory and describe its relevance for companies that scale new products and services. They write:

> "Disruption" describes a process whereby a smaller company with fewer resources is able to successfully challenge established incumbent businesses. Specifically, as incumbents focus on improving their products and services for their most demanding (and usually most profitable) customers, they exceed the needs of some segments and ignore the needs of others. Entrants that prove disruptive begin by successfully targeting those overlooked segments, gaining a foothold by delivering more-suitable functionality—frequently at a lower price. Incumbents, chasing higher profitability in more-demanding segments, tend not to respond vigorously. Entrants then move upmarket, delivering the performance that incumbents' mainstream customers require, while preserving the advantages that drove their early success. When mainstream customers start adopting the entrants' offerings in volume, disruption has occurred.[8]

Christiansen and his co-authors remind readers that markets are divided into segments with different types of customers. In mature industries, the big players often neglect the lower-end markets because they perceive them to be less lucrative. (Think about low-cost bottles of wine compared to expensive labels. Who wouldn't want to sell the most expensive bottles of wine?) But on closer inspection, there is actually a very large market for sensibly priced products.

What is true for wine and software is also true for social impact goods and services. The 80/20 rule reminds innovators to always look for the *unmet needs of customers and communities*, wherever they are. Rather than creating products or services that satisfy *all* the wants and needs of a small subset of customers, organizations would be better advised to satisfy *most* of the wants and needs of customers, provided they do so at a lower overall cost to the consumer. This is the secret to massively scaling innovations with social and environmental benefits.

Nine Conditions for Scaling

Effective scaling relates to product design and a good theory of change. But it also requires appropriate business conditions, as well as initiatives that have been carefully vetted and provide real value to customers. The following section presents nine essential business conditions for scaling, based on our research and experience in the social impact sector. Think of this as a checklist of best practices for organizations that are considering rolling out scalable, data-driven solutions to new audiences.

1. Is There a Substantial Market?

This book has emphasized the importance of designing innovations that address the needs of *real communities*. If you are designing a social innovation that has the potential for true impact, you'll want to gather quality data about the effectiveness of your initiative so that stakeholders can determine if scaling represents a true business opportunity. Scaling is not something that an organization can experiment with via trial-and-error methods. Effective scaling requires resources and a sustained commitment from your organization. Research shows that organizations that commit to scaling will require additional budget, staff, resources, and organizational support. However, when organizations invest these resources they tend to produce more predictable outcomes than organizations which only commit to "experimenting around the edges" or "sending up trial balloons" to determine the feasibility of new initiatives.[9]

To think strategically about scaling opportunities, conduct a *market landscape analysis* as part of your discernment process. A market landscape analysis will help you determine who the potential customers or clients are for your product, what their needs and characteristics will be, as well as the competitive ecosystem in your industry. In some cases, there will be a *service desert* in the community where you have the ability to provide a useful good or service. It could be a systemic challenge such as homelessness, mental illness, addiction, underemployment, financial challenges, or food instability. However, a landscape analysis may also reveal that your region has many quality solutions available to residents. Adding another service might offer *incremental benefits* to the community, but it is more likely that partnering with another organization would be a better approach than adding another option through a new service. Since creating and scaling a new innovation is expensive and time-consuming, it is usually better to collaborate with others rather than foisting a redundant solution on clients or customers.

The human services nonprofit sector in the U.S. is extremely large. According to IRS data aggregated by Giving Compass Insights, there were 313,000 human services organizations active in 2022. This included more than 16,000 organizations supporting a homeless population of 550,000 people; over 12,000 organizations supporting 12 million households facing food insecurity; and 31,000 organizations addressing substance abuse, addiction, and mental health issues.[10] Before an organization creates a new social services initiative, it behooves them to study the marketplace carefully and understand what is unique about their value proposition. The same is true for social impact initiatives in healthcare, education, environmental causes, and other impact categories. Your organization can do this research by reviewing academic journals, government reports, conference proceedings, and the publications of advocacy groups, or by downloading custom landscape reports from organizations like Giving Compass Insights. Although some of the custom reports cost money, they can be huge time-savers. The Giving Compass Insights reports aggregate hundreds of thousands of government records and quickly identify partnership prospects, service deserts, and opportunities related to the UN SDGs.

2. How Strong is Your Theory of Change?

As we discussed in Chapter 6, a theory of change is the empirical basis underlying a proposed social innovation. A theory of change explains how your proposed solution will address environmental concerns or community challenges and be validated through data collection. In many organizations, however, a theory of change vision takes shape slowly. Organizations tend to articulate well what they do, but not how or why they do it. This trial-and-error approach to innovation becomes a problem when organizations want to scale their projects.

To develop a robust theory of change, be sure your rationale provides specific details about how and why the innovation produces benefits. Clarify the types of activities required to produce these outcomes, and be sure to detail the roles and responsibilities of service recipients, donors, funders, staff, and community members.[11]

If conditions are expected to be different in new markets, the theory of change needs to explain how and why the intervention will still work in new settings. Appropriate data-gathering methods should also be put in place so that reliable data can be gathered when the project goes to scale. This may mean upgrading software systems or preparing to use a common data model to store and share information. (For more about the benefits of a common data model, see Chapter 7.)

A social impact project that is scaled should align clearly with the *strengths* and *reputation* of an organization. Although businesses traditionally look for ways to expand into new markets, customers recognize when an organization is simply profit seeking or experimenting in an area they are inexperienced with. On the other hand, when an organization expands into a space they are recognized in and trusted for, there is a higher likelihood that new products or services will be accepted. This is because dependable organizations build trust with consumers. They identify problems and look for opportunities that arise from ongoing work and service.[12] Your theory of change can include these dynamics, too, as you leverage the existing strengths of a brand or organization to deliver value.

A useful example of this can be drawn from the sustainability initiatives of Footprint, a materials science company we introduced in Chapter 6. Footprint was founded in 2014 to eliminate the single-use and short-term use of plastics in product packaging. The company recognized that plastic products were having an adverse effect on human beings, waterways, wildlife, and natural habitats around the globe. Much of this pollution was unnecessary, because there were inexpensive alternatives to plastics in food packaging, medical waste, shopping bags, plastic bottles, bubble wrap, agricultural products, and more. The company decided to invest in scientific research, so that they could propose alternatives to single-use plastics. They also wanted to spread the word about plastic pollution and plastic alternatives. Recognizing that they faced an uphill battle, they sought strategic partnerships with a range of organizations to spark a global movement around sustainable packaging. They aspired to design and manufacture solutions with environmental benefits, then transform leading sectors of the economy around the transition from plastics to alternatives.

Susan Koehler was the Chief Marketing Officer (CMO) of Footprint from 2019 to 2022. Her innovation challenge was to scale a comprehensive marketing message so that it would raise awareness about single-use plastics and change consumer behavior within sectors of the economy that had never considered the problem before. Her teams started their work by creating promotions that would encourage individual consumers to monitor and reduce their plastic usage. Among these promotions were "Plastic Free July" and "Pledge 2050." Pledge 2050 was particularly innovative; it asked individuals and companies to pledge that they would significantly reduce their usage of plastic bags, utensils, straws, and water bottles. If consumers took the pledge now, they could see the collective impact their use of alternatives would amount to by the year 2050.

Next, Susan sought corporate partners to leverage and amplify the sustainability message. Footprint approached the ownership group of the Phoenix Suns, the men's NBA team, and asked for the naming rights to the popular basketball stadium. In addition, Footprint asked the stadium operations staff if they would be willing to completely eliminate single-use plastics from their facility. When Footprint Center opened in Phoenix, Arizona, in 2021, it rolled out a new assortment of products and packaging materials, pledging that there would be no single-use plastic water bottles, straws, bags, or utensils in the stadium. The facility also featured recycling and compost containers, not trash cans, to facilitate a recycling loop from plant-based alternatives to renewable products.[13] Thousands of people learned first-hand at concerts and events how easy it could be to introduce sustainable materials and practices to an organization. The next year, the Phoenix Suns received the NBA Changemaker of the Year Award from the NBA owners, industry recognition that Susan and her teams have leveraged to promote sustainability initiatives in the National Football League, International Olympic Committee, U.S. Olympic Committee, Formula E auto racing, and more. What started as an innovative campaign to reduce single-use plastics has become a global sustainability movement designed to reform the sports and entertainment industries.

3. Do You Have a Solid Revenue Model?

Every social impact organization needs a revenue model. When design teams propose a new product or service, they often suggest potential revenue models that leaders and stakeholders might consider to fund their innovations. But before you scale your project or initiative, it is important that you carefully vet these ideas and select the revenue model that has the best chance of maximizing income and resource utilization in your organization. A *revenue model* is a business plan for making the product or service financially sustainable, a crucial requirement for both nonprofit and for-profit organizations. Throughout this book, we have highlighted the benefits of the business-to-business (B2B) revenue model, as well as software-as-a-service (SaaS) models in tech for good companies. B2B and SaaS are schemes that can work well for organizations that plan to market digital services over the Internet. However, there are a number of compelling revenue models. We summarize them here briefly, recognizing there are additional options you might want to consider, including hybrid models that mix and match these schemes.[14]

The first is a *self-sustaining revenue model*, in which customers pay for the new product or service, providing the organization with sufficient revenue to cover the operating costs of the product plus surplus revenue to compensate staff and allow for expansion.

The *cross-subsidization model*, often used by organizations that have a range of products and services, allows customers to fund operations by buying the most established products, which subsidizes new product offerings until they also become self-sustaining.

The *grant-supported, fee-for-service model* allows customers to purchase products and serves at below cost, but then the organization solicits grants or donations to cover the remaining costs, including staff compensation and money set aside for new initiatives. The grant-supported model is typical in social service organizations where clients cannot afford to pay the market rate for services such as meals, hygiene, healthcare, counseling, education, or job training.

Finally, an organization may be entirely dependent on *grant-funded support* for their initiatives. In this revenue model, an organization does not charge customers or clients for services at all, or their "product" is not commercially aligned but related to information distribution, campaigning, or advocacy. Grant-funded initiatives are considered financially sustainable if adequate funding can be secured in advance from partner organizations, government sources, grant writing, foundations, or private philanthropy.

Determining the best revenue model for a product or service is essential before an organization makes the commitment to scaling its operations. Since scaling naturally incurs costs, both in product creation and distribution, it is important to have a solid revenue model before the go-to-market campaign begins.

4. Economic Conditions

So far in this chapter, we've discussed business conditions within organizations and the social impact sector. However, it is also important to consider external economic conditions and the broader financial climate to understand how a new innovation might be received or adopted by consumers, who are also impacted by macro-economic issues. These conditions include the inflationary rate, the unemployment rate, the interest rate for loans, currency exchange rates, health and pandemic scenarios, and general economic output measures, such as a country's gross domestic product (GDP).

As we saw in 2022 and 2023, the inflationary rate and unemployment rate have dramatic impacts on global financial markets, compensation schemes, foreclosure rates, business loans, national politics, and more. If economic conditions are perceived to be stagnant or declining, it's typically harder to raise capital, expand a business, and solicit financial support from donors. If economic conditions are perceived to be good, customers and donors tend to spend more on goods and services, including the infrastructure for social impact projects. A curious variation in this formula takes place when certain businesses or organizations thrive under *adverse conditions*. For example, during the Covid-19 pandemic, online shopping retailers such as Amazon.com posted record earnings, and digital streaming services saw significant growth and expansion. This took place because most consumers were sequestered at home, and they spent their days streaming content and shopping online. However, fewer students went to university during the pandemic, and many people delayed or avoided healthcare appointments and medical screenings. These gaps in service delivery led to adverse education and health effects on global populations, as well as financial challenges for many organizations.

The question is: What will economic conditions be like in the future, and how might social innovators respond to them? While macroeconomic trends are difficult to predict, it is useful to recognize that economic conditions can powerfully affect the *standard of living* in human communities and therefore content and demand for social innovations. Economic conditions also impact supply chains, the availability of resources, prospects for funding and donations, and the timing of social impact interventions and campaigns. If you plan to scale a new social innovation, be sure your theory of change aligns with economic trends.

5. Can You Lower the Cost of Your Product or Service?

The promise of scaling is that it *reduces* the unit cost of a product or service while simultaneously raising revenues and overall impact. Under normal operating conditions, an organization that expands its operations by adding manufacturing costs, support staff, and overhead doesn't necessarily do this. More typically, an iterative growth scheme brings in additional revenue while expanding the organization's financial footprint. But scaling is an *exponential growth strategy*. It tries to increase revenues and impact *without* substantially increasing staff or overhead.

The goal is to accelerate impact by reaching new people and markets while keeping costs low.

In reality, this type of revenue efficiency can be hard to achieve. Before you plan to scale your operation, determine if you can truly lower the cost of producing your product or service without substantially increasing overhead. In addition, you'll need to lower costs while keeping product quality high (or meeting the 80/20 rule for major market segments). On the ethics side, scaling should not be an invitation to demand more from your employees without giving them additional resources or compensation. Instead, scaling is an efficiency puzzle wrapped in social and financial constraints. When conditions are right, organizations can ferret out hidden costs in the system and leverage creative solutions.

Recall the Desirable/Feasible/Viable diagram we discussed in Chapter 5 (Figure 5.1). Now is the time to focus again on the practical constraints of viability and feasibility in your innovation. While it is important to address the needs of actual clients and communities, it is imperative to achieve this within the limits of technical systems and ethical guidelines. Ask yourself these questions: "Will this new innovation be sustainable for our organization to offer?" "Will a sufficient audience be able to pay for it?" "Are there features that we could remove from our product without losing substantial value?" "Are there other revenue models for our product, such as a scenario in which a partner organization pays for a portion of the cost?" "Can we move from a single-purchase model to a subscription model, reducing the likelihood that customers will discontinue our service?"

When reducing costs, you can either reduce the per-unit cost of your product or service (leveraging economies of scale), or you can find a way to increase demand (perhaps by retaining more customers or addressing new markets). Both strategies can lower net costs, which is important if you want to produce a product on a massive scale. If net costs go up, scaling is not financially viable, despite the social good that may result from the intervention. In the best of all worlds, you will attract a consortium of skilled and well-funded partners to your project, allowing each organization to contribute according to their strengths and expertise. We explore an example of this type of scaling below, related to the challenge to defeat malaria.

6. Is Scaling Environmentally Sustainable?

In the eighteenth and nineteenth centuries, conversations about scaling (or economies of scale) surfaced few concerns about environmental sustainability. The invention of iron production and the steam engine sped up the industrialization process, which led to the development of railroads, steamships, industrial factories, and numerous innovations that raised living standards and boosted prosperity. However, there was little consideration about the environmental consequences of these achievements. Governments, industrialists, and factory workers paid little attention to the depletion of natural resources, pollution, habitat destruction, or the health consequences of industrialization. The general belief was that the planet's natural resources were inexhaustible.

The fragile condition of our planet is now daily news. This means that social entrepreneurs need to build into their operating procedures a commitment to carefully steward the resources of people *and* planet as they build scalable, data-driven solutions for customers and communities. The term "responsible business" has been used recently to capture some of this commitment to sustainability, and you'll see it in the mission statements of numerous corporations, especially in Europe and North America. *Responsible business* means that an organization has taken the ethical responsibility to consider social, economic, and environmental factors as they scale products and conduct regular business activity. Responsible businesses commit to being driven by motivations other than profit for shareholders. They commit to safeguarding the planet by advocating for environmentally safe, ethical, and inclusive working conditions, products, and initiatives. B Corporation (B Corp) certification, based on corporate commitments and social and environmental performance, is a related standard that has arisen for sustainable business activity in for-profit corporations. Kin + Carta is an example of a company with B Corp certification and a commitment to social and environmental performance.

The need to consider sustainable practices is most obvious when we about how much of the world creates consumer products. For example, approximately 90 percent of the toys manufactured in the world today are made from plastic, despite the environmental problems associated with this material. It is important to ask several questions related to sustainability, especially when scaling a product or service: "What steps can we take to ensure that our social innovations are as sustainable as possible?" "Can social impact organizations be leaders in reducing waste, reusing goods, and promoting sustainable practices?" "Are there ways we can support our employees so that the workplace cultivates a sense of well-being and is more socially sustainable?"

7. Has Your Organization Considered All Market Conditions?

We've all probably observed a restaurant chain that does splendidly in one part of town but seems to struggle in other locations. Although the food is the same, market conditions are somehow different in the new location, and the attempt to replicate the business eventually fails.

Why is this? One of the challenges with scaling is the vexing issue of hidden market conditions that conspire to reduce the effectiveness of replication and growth. Social innovators need to consider this problem carefully, even if they are not selling fine-dining experiences. There are a number of reasons why conditions will vary subtly as you move from one market context to the next. The first is *product presentation or quality issues*, meaning that the components or "ingredients" in a product or client experience are subtly different from one location to the next. In online contexts, this happens when a smartphone app or media product is presented in different ways depending on the platform customers are using. For example, a podcast series will appear differently on different platforms, and the way a customer buys or plays a media product will change from location to location.

There can also be differences in how *employees or agents provide services* from one location or context to the next. This is because tacit knowledge about products and services is passed along via oral methods much of the time. Training is different between social service offices or tutoring centers. Management structures are altered. Something about the organization's chemistry or messaging is somehow different from place to place. As a solution, try creating manuals, training systems, and procedures that will draw out what makes your organization special before you scale it elsewhere.

The *needs of the intended customers or beneficiaries* of a product are often different from location to location. These regional factors don't tend to surface in prototype or initial product testing, because assumptions are made about who the "ideal users" of a product are. (You can't test it on everyone.) But subtle differences in how users operate products sometimes leads to a product or initiative falling flat when it is deployed in a new area. This is why we recommend human-centered design approaches, deep community engagement, and continual testing and refinement for new social innovations. Capture data that *proves* you are making a positive change in the community, and then have at least one independent verification of these results from a different community or customer base that confirms your theory of change.

8. Do You Have the Capacity for Sustained Impact?

An organization that is planning to launch a new product or initiative needs to be prepared to support the innovation over the long term. This means it will be necessary to plan for gradual expansion in the organization. Note that it may not be required to lease more office space or construct new buildings. Many tech for good organizations operate just fine remotely or in a hybrid manner, which reduces the need for physical space when the organization scales. But you will need to fund appropriate technology (IT systems and personnel), customer support systems, and sales personnel that can help the organization sell the product or service. You'll also need to acquire appropriate software to disseminate information and tools to organize data, particularly the tracking data that you can use to verify your theory of change and establish success metrics. By focusing on internal structures and people, you'll be prepared for expansion before it happens.

Also remember that the employees in social impact organizations need care and support, because they are ultimately the most valuable assets within the company. They enact the mission of the organization and need to be engaged with any new initiatives the leadership team is planning. There are different growth models you can use for staffing up. For example, rather than building physical infrastructure or hiring employees, an organization may choose to leverage the *network* of a partner for product distribution, marketing, and assessment.

An excellent example of the network model is the National Institutes of Health (NIH), an agency within the U.S. government that developed a diabetes prevention program that reduced the incidence of Type 2 diabetes by 58 percent in at-risk individuals.[15] This social innovation had great potential to improve public health, but the NIH did not have the resources to build new teaching facilities or hire employees to deliver the curriculum nationwide. Instead, the NIH evaluated community resources across the U.S. and discovered that 60 percent of Americans live within three miles of a YMCA. The NIH partnered with local community college instructors and the YMCA to deliver the curriculum, and it was financially supported by regional health insurers that agreed to reimburse program costs. Although the NIH had to modify its initial design to adapt to the new scaling model, they tested the system carefully and modified their theory of change to include network partners. When the health initiative was publicly evaluated in 2013, there were 614 locations across the U.S. where the diabetes program was active.[16] The scaling and replication program was successful.

9. Have You Fully Exploited Digital Transformation for Operational Efficiency?

In Chapter 3, we described *digital transformation* as the process of integrating digital technology into all areas of a business operation to add value and build capacity for future operations. When social impact firms begin this work, they indicate to potential partners that they are ready to share data and deliver products and services using the most efficient methods. Digital transformation implies operational efficiency and readiness for purpose-driven work. It doesn't always mean a company is using the most expensive technology. It simply means that traditional ways of doing business have been replaced by streamlined systems and procedures. This includes how groups function internally and handle business tasks like interacting with clients, gathering data, communicating internally, managing the supply chain, and reporting to stakeholders.

When an organization is preparing to scale a new product or service, they should return to the same digital readiness questions:

- How can we improve our product with digital-first methods?
- How can we gather data and quickly respond to changing market conditions?
- How can emerging technology systems help us do this work?

At its core, digital transformation is a way to standardize operations and use resources efficiently. This means using computer systems rather than paper; gathering data to evaluate product effectiveness; analyzing the data in real time; managing inventory and the supply chain; keeping data secure; and treating customers well. Computers have their downsides. But they can also automate many processes effectively, store data inexpensively, and allow for portable, mobile business operations.

Using cloud computing and Internet technologies has become essential, especially within tech for good organizations. Cloud-computing scenarios allow users to have a similar customer experience in a web browser across numerous locations. Digital solutions can be created, revised, distributed, and updated via one central website or server, then shared globally. This makes replication possible and supports a unified theory of change across different markets. Organizations still need to meet customer expectations in online scenarios, and thoughtfully adapt human contact to online experiences, which can be challenging. Training, infrastructure, and security challenges also require professional IT solutions that take time and resources. But it's striking how many social impact organizations have taken to these challenges and emerged as major players in the global digital ecosystem, thriving in the roles as digital-first, multinational corporations.

Digitization also means using existing systems and networks more effectively to help the organization reduce costs and distribute innovative solutions. This involves using low-cost tools and infrastructures that already exist, including laptops, smartphone networks, social media, cloud-based solutions, free Wi-Fi, public work spaces, and so on. In each context, technology is the efficient mechanism that connects social impact organizations to clients and customers, making commerce rapid and efficient. The more elements of a program that can be standardized before scaling, the better.

Scaling Through Creative Partnerships

We conclude this chapter with a case study that demonstrates the power of scaling through creative partnerships. A campaign demonstrating this approach took shape in 2008, when an assortment of multilateral agencies, nonprofit organizations, pharmaceutical companies, foundations, and scientists partnered to reduce the deadly impact of malaria around the world. The consortium convened to create the Global Malaria Action Plan, which strengthened existing healthcare systems, searched for cures, and coordinated a multinational response to the disease.[17]

Malaria is challenging to stamp out, because the malaria parasite carried by mosquitos is resistant to drugs and spurred on by changing environmental conditions, such as rising temperatures, flooding, and civil war. It is particularly devastating for young children. In 2008, approximately 243 million cases of fever and 863,000 deaths were reported worldwide, mostly in Africa.[18] Recognizing the systemic nature of the challenge, the Bill & Melinda Gates Foundation decided to partner in fighting the disease. Their strategic plan involved developing new anti-malaria vaccines, deploying therapeutic drugs and diagnostics, expanding the use of mosquito nets and insecticide, and advocating for effective policies and financing.[19] At the time, Jeff Raikes, a former Microsoft executive, was the CEO of the Gates Foundation. He led the team in developing a plan to scale a global response to the challenge.

The consortium worked within typical innovation constraints: They needed to find a solution that saved lives but also conformed to the limits of desirability, feasibility, and viability. No one organization had the resources to scale a comprehensive solution to the problem. However, the Gates Foundation played a convening role, partnering with the global organization PATH to support the Malaria

Vaccine Initiative; collaborating on the Medicines for Malaria Venture, which developed therapeutic drugs; sponsoring field trials for mosquito nets with the Innovative Vector Control Consortium; and publicizing the initiative at the 2010 FIFA Men's World Cup in South Africa, educating over one million supporters about the global fight against malaria. Collectively, the Gates Foundation contributed over $259 million to funding these efforts, describing their work as convening, leveraging key partnerships, and providing *catalytic philanthropy*, an emerging framework for global impact partnerships.[20]

Collectively, the consortium developed several vaccines and drugs, and financed the purchase of millions of doses in the hardest-hit countries. The Gates Foundation didn't formulate the vaccines on their own, but funded pharmaceutical companies and scientists to supervise the research and field testing. Through the healthcare company Novartis, they distributed 42 million doses of life-saving drugs in 32 countries. They also distributed millions of mosquito nets and related vector-control tools. By 2015, the global initiative was producing tangible results, a trend that continued for almost a decade until the Covid-19 pandemic disrupted operations and caused malaria rates to rise. Globally, malaria deaths declined steadily from 864,000 in 2000 to 586,000 in 2015 and to 576,000 in 2019. Collectively, an estimated 2.1 billion malaria cases and 11.7 million malaria deaths were averted in the period 2000–2022.[21]

The collaborative solution points the way to a time when malaria will be eradicated worldwide, despite the complex transmission patterns of the disease. This is not a "perfect" solution, because the disease is so challenging, and one solution does not fit every country or setting. Behind the numbers are obvious pain points, including stories of hardship, suffering, and tragedy. But partnership and scaling methodologies have lowered costs, saved lives, and reduced human suffering in ways that global health officials previously thought impossible.

Raikes summarized the Gates Foundation's approach in 2010:

> We take on these types of investments in conjunction with a wide number of partners. While we are a large foundation, in the type of work that we're doing we represent a small percentage of the overall funding. Global Alliance for Vaccine Initiatives has reached more than 250 million children with vaccines, and that requires the commitment not just of the Gates Foundation but also of a large number of donor countries and other partners. In terms of scale, we always think how we can effectively use our resources in conjunction with others in order to achieve those big aspirations.[22]

Scaling increased the magnitude and reach of the project, so that it had a deeper, more sustained impact on real-world communities. Regardless of the context, however, scaling is a tool that allows a business or nonprofit organization to do more of what it is good at, extending its reach into new areas and contexts.

In the next chapter, we focus on emerging opportunities in the social impact sector related to artificial intelligence (AI) technology. We explain what AI is and how Conversational AI systems such as ChatGPT have changed the landscape for social impact work. We explore ethical approaches to AI and how organizations can use AI to support environmental causes, humanitarian initiatives, accessibility, healthcare, and more. We conclude with a case study featuring a tech for good company that uses bee pollen to move forward biodiversity and clean air initiatives.

Notes

1 Christian Seelos and Johanna Mair, *Innovation and Scaling for Impact: How Social Enterprises Do It* (Stanford, CA: Stanford Business Books, 2017), 5.
2 Bill Drayton, "Everyone a Changemaker," *Peer Review*, vol. 7, no. 3 (Gale Academic OneFile, 2005). https://link.gale.com/apps/doc/A134477247/AONE?u=taco36403&sid=bookmark-AONE&xid=-ed5d65c6. Accessed April 7, 2024.
3 Jeffrey L. Bradach, "Going to Scale: The Challenge of Replicating Social Programs," *Stanford Social Innovation Review* (Spring 2003), 19.
4 Jeffrey Bradach and Abe Grindle. "Transformative Scale: The Future of Growing What Works." *Stanford Social Innovation Review* (February 19, 2014). https://doi.org/10.48558/16TY-KS73. Accessed December 5, 2023.
5 Seelos and Mair, *Innovation and Scaling for Impact*, 31.
6 Bradach, "Going to Scale: The Challenge of Replicating Social Programs," 21.
7 Clayton Christensen, *The Innovator's Dilemma: When New Technologies Cause Great Firms to Fail* (Boston, MA: Harvard Business Review Press, 1997). For a recent book that discusses these themes and their relation to capitalism and the world economy, see Philippe Aghion, Céline Antonin, and Simon Bunel, *The Power of Creative Destruction: Economic Upheaval and the Wealth of Nations* (Cambridge, MA: Harvard University Press, 2021).
8 Clayton M. Christensen, Michael E. Raynor, and Rory McDonald, "What Is Disruptive Innovation?" *Harvard Business Review* (December 2015). https://hbr.org/2015/12/what-is-disruptive-innovation. Accessed December 5, 2023
9 Seelos and Mair, *Innovation and Scaling for Impact*, 37.
10 Giving Compass Insights summary data current as of December 5, 2023. See https://x4i.org/us-nonprofit-landscape-human-services-insights.

11 Bradach, "Going to Scale: The Challenge of Replicating Social Programs," 20.

12 Seelos and Mair, *Innovation and Scaling for Impact*, 30.

13 "Phoenix Suns and Mercury Form Global Partnership for Newly Named Footprint Center to become a Transformative Venue to Accelerate a Plastic-Free Future" (July 15, 2021). www.nba.com/suns/footprintcenter. Accessed December 5, 2023.

14 The terminology used for these summaries comes from Teresa Chahine, *Social Entrepreneurship: Building Impact Step by Step*, Second Edition (New York: Routledge, 2023), 136–41.

15 Case study described in Bradach and Grindle, "Transformative Scale: The Future of Growing What Works."

16 Kristen V. Brown, "YMCA Diabetes Prevention Program May Be U.S. Model," *San Francisco Chronicle* (September 5, 2013).

17 Roll Back Malaria Partnership, *Global Malaria Action Plan* (Geneva: Roll Back Malaria Partnership, 2008), 13.

18 Bill & Melinda Gates Foundation, "Malaria Strategy Overview" (Seattle, WA, 2011), 1. https://docs.gatesfoundation.org/Documents/malaria-strategy.pdf. Accessed December 5, 2023.

19 Gates Foundation, "Malaria Strategy Overview," 2–4.

20 "Catalytic philanthropy cuts through … divisions by stimulating cross-sector collaborations and mobilizing stakeholders to create shared solutions. Building alliances that create the conditions for a solution to emerge and take hold is a very different pursuit from the usual grantmaking process of trying to direct funds to the one organization that offers the most appealing approach." For more about catalytic approaches, including procedures at the Gates Foundation, see Mark R. Kramer, "Catalytic Philanthropy." *Stanford Social Innovation Review*, vol. 7, no. 4 (2009), 30–35. https://doi.org/10.48558/YKDQ-NS59. Accessed December 5, 2023.

21 World Health Organization, *World Malaria Report 2023* (Geneva: World Health Organization, 2023), xix. www.who.int/publications/i/item/9789240086173. Accessed December 5, 2023.

22 Interview with Jeff Raikes, *Alliance Magazine* (June 1, 2010). www.alliancemagazine.org/interview/interview-jeff-raikes. Accessed December 5, 2023.

9 AI for Good

What do bees have to do with AI? You could say that one buzzes and the other is a buzzword. Clever turns of phrase aside, you're going to hear exactly how honeybees are connected to AI in this chapter.

To conclude *This Little World*, we'll share some insights and perspective about the growing landscape of AI solutions in the social impact sector. We're aware of the futile nature of this exercise. Capturing a butterfly in a tsunami is an apt description of the fervent pace of AI advancements swirling around us these days, and the pace of change is dizzying at times. We don't mind the tempest. The winds force us to get outside. Just don't forget to smell the roses or watch the clouds blow by while you walk.

Advancements in artificial intelligence and machine learning are rapidly outpacing the marketplace's ability to adapt. But since Michael Halvorson is an historian and Shelly Cano Kurtz is an entrepreneur and risk taker, we're going to roll the dice and hope this benefits you as you continue your journey as a social innovator. One of our overarching principles is to educate ourselves so that we can be in conversation with people who like to solve challenging problems.

With so much fear, confusion, and public discourse related to this topic, we simply plan to document this moment in time, highlight some trusted sources, and try to inspire you with ideas about how AI is supporting social impact organizations. We'll share expert takeaways from academics, entrepreneurs, and practitioners from companies such as Kin + Carta, Microsoft, SAS, Witty Works, AI4SP, and BeeOdiversity, the startup that uses bee pollen for biodiversity and clean air initiatives.

We won't be covering AI from A to Z, but we'll do our best to paint this moment in history with a social innovator's brush. If we're successful, you'll get a summary of how AI is evolving, along with tangible examples about using AI to accelerate positive social outcomes.

First, we'll take a look at the AI for Good movement, which is using Generative and Conversational AI, and interesting use cases

DOI: 10.4324/9781003465669-9

that show positive impact for people, the planet, or both. We'll discuss how purpose-driven organizations use AI for mission delivery, while pointing out the value of developing ethical frameworks and guardrails for protection against threats and misinformation. Before we dive in, let's also clarify a bit of syntax. In this book, we've adopted the accepted practice of capitalizing Artificial Intelligence when referring to the field of practice and this discipline of study, but we use lowercase to refer to the general concept. The accepted acronym is simply AI.

The AI for Good Movement

The United States has the world's third highest population with basic access to digital technology, a figure corresponding to basic Internet access for eight out of every ten Americans as of late 2023. This figure drops to about six out of ten people globally, although precise estimates about digital access are challenging. Nonetheless, considering the audience for this book, there is a high likelihood that you have an Internet-enabled device nearby—it might be even be in your hand right now. You could use it to ask a number of probing questions about artificial intelligence, if you wanted—probably without even typing the letters. (Most smartphones are equipped with voice recognition tools that replace or augment typing.) If you do so, you'll find that AI is a massive topic. As of the printing of this book, typing "artificial intelligence" in a Google.com search resulted in 1.5 billion results. That's billion with a "b."

Few popular topics related to computing have engendered this much interest, this fast, on our planet. Even the Y2K problem—a global panic about software reliability that took place in the build-up to the year 2000—did not spark this much discussion. As Michael pointed out back in 1999, there's probably no good reason to prepare for the transition by holing up in a mine shaft with stocks of grain, ammunition, and barter goods.[1] Y2K was mostly a non-event, and much of our anxiety about AI might be misplaced, too. In both cases, the main psychological driver seems to be anxiety about the unknown, paired with a general fear of technological innovation.

How "Good" is AI for Good?

Although we have used the term "tech for good" throughout the book to capture the importance of skill development and our lived experience, we support the general consensus that technology is neither good nor evil. Instead, it is a reflection of our global society, with its many hopes, dreams, and worries.[2] A recent book that captures this sentiment is *Tools and Weapons: The Promise and the Peril of the Digital Age*, by Brad Smith and Carol Ann Browne, originally published in 2019 and updated in 2021.[3] Basically, the same logic about corporate responsibility and digital transformation applies to artificial intelligence and its capabilities. Like a hammer, AI can be used to build or destroy. You will have to draw your own conclusions about which human characteristics will be emphasized, enhanced, or extended. Scholarly opinions vary about the potential benefits and consequences of AI, as a survey of recent books shows.[4] But in one form or several, AI is here to stay. Moving forward, we choose hopeful optimism as an outlook. But to plan for a good future with AI-enabled technologies, we must be honest about the risks and challenges.

AI as a discipline of computer science is at least 70 years old. In 1970, MIT scientist Marvin Minsky told *Life Magazine*, "from three to eight years we will have a machine with the general intelligence of an average human being."[5] However, the challenges of simulating abstract thought, processing human language, and self-recognition were more difficult than Minsky initially thought. In the years since then, AI research has proliferated into numerous subfields, including machine learning, robotics, expert systems, computer vision, natural language processing, ethics, and more. The work has been taking place behind the scenes in research labs for decades. The newest breakthroughs, Generative AI and Conversational AI, are simply grabbing the headlines—and for good reason. Generative AI is a type of AI that produces useful content, such as text or images. Conversational AI is a type of AI that can simulate human conversation, such as ChatGPT. We'll emphasize these two applications in the sections that follow, and leave the other fields to AI scholars.

In the world of business, the renewed interest in AI has led to a number of important global conferences on the subject. It is encouraging to see how the philanthropy and social impact sectors are taking the lead in what is being called the "AI for Good" movement, where thought leaders gather to discuss how AI can address pressing social and environmental issues. In 2023, Shelly attended a session entitled "AI for Good: Revolutionizing Philanthropy with Innovative Solutions,"[6] hosted by Fluxx, a nonprofit grant management platform, and PEAK, the nonprofit membership organization introduced in Chapter 6.

The virtual session was attended by 570 representatives from philanthropic organizations and nonprofit grantees, demonstrating the huge need for guidance and training on the subject. The presenters highlighted four key themes that have become clarion calls in the AI for Good movement:

- Cybersecurity considerations
- Responsible AI
- Representation
- Emphasizing "humanity first" principles

We begin our discussion of AI for Good by discussing these themes. They are closely connected to the ethical considerations that social innovators should follow when they design, test, and market new solutions powered by artificial intelligence.

First, cybersecurity is an obvious concern for corporations, governments, and individual users. This lengthy topic could encompass an entire book. Suffice it to say that cybersecurity is an arms race of sorts between offenders (hackers and scammers) and defenders (governments, organizations, and individuals). AI-fueled attacks can lead to data breaches, data tampering, and sophisticated network assaults. But threats of this type have already been an aspect of cybersecurity preparation in cloud computing, data management, and social media contexts. Until advanced protective measures and tools are in place, however, there is room for caution. Even then, it's always a good idea to "trust, but verify," as Ronald Reagan was fond of saying during disarmament talks.

"Responsible AI" is also a leading concern. The professional services company Accenture defines Responsible AI as "the practice of designing, developing, and deploying AI with good intention to empower employees and businesses, and fairly impact customers and society—allowing companies to engender trust and scale AI with confidence."[7] This vision emphasizes the *ethical use* of artificial intelligence for people and the planet, and opens up a key opportunity (and responsibility) for social innovators and entrepreneurs. AI is for everyone, so businesses that use AI need to be mindful of diversity and inclusion issues as they elevate human needs. AI should inspire trust and benefit all people, not just those motivated by power or profit.

Representation also matters, meaning that a diverse group of employees, citizens, and identities is depicted in data gathered and processed by AI tools. We started this chapter with the statistic that 8 out of 10 Americans enjoy some level of digital connectivity, a number that drops to 6 out of 10 people worldwide. This means that many people, organizations, and communities are still not online or accessing global information resources. For AI systems to be the most effective, we need to get more people with access to the Internet. Even when communities are online, they may not be willing (or able) to participate in sharing data or using AI-powered applications. While it is appropriate for some people to "opt out" because of concerns over privacy or a lack of perceived benefit, it is critical that our information networks safely represent everyone. This includes the young, the elderly, and the disabled. (For more about social innovation in this space, see Chapter 4.)

Finally, the AI for Good movement emphasizes "humanity first" principles. Let's remember that AI was created by humans. Kerrin Mitchell, Co-Founder and Chief Development Officer at Fluxx, offers a helpful definition of what it means to be human in this context. She defines humanity using four truths:

1. The human race includes everyone on Earth.
2. Humans shape perspectives on Earth and evolve nature.
3. Humans have the ability to make sophisticated tools.
4. Humans are not robots.

AI for Good systems need to recognize these core characteristics and build on decades of interdisciplinary research from around the globe.

The AI for Good movement is fueled by a range of companies that are focusing on positive solutions for humanity. An important goal of these organizations is to reduce the anxiety created by emerging technologies and make them useful.

Make the World Work Better

Kin + Carta is a global consulting company with this vision that has the additional distinction of being the first certified B Corporation (B Corp) to be publicly traded on the London Stock Exchange. B Corps are charged with demonstrating their value and impact not just to shareholders, but to employees, customers, the environment, and society. The Kin + Carta team, led by CEO Kelly Manthey, consists of 2,000 global engineers, data scientists, and strategists focused on sustainable yet profitable approaches to problem-solving. While they don't exclusively focus on social innovation, their company ethos is built on a foundation of social impact and using business as a force for good. As a triple bottom line company, they align priorities equally between people, the planet, and profit. Their motto is "Make the world work better, for everyone."

One of the leaders at Kin + Carta is Cameron Turner, Vice President of Data Science. Turner had a distinguished career at Microsoft and also built a successful AI startup that used cloud-based machine learning to accelerate data-driven decision making and digital transformation in companies. Turner is well positioned to advise the industry on best practices for exploring and using AI. There have been some amazing success stories at Kin + Carta, including modernizing rail travel, boosting agricultural production, and enhancing the fan experience at soccer games.

However, there is more than a little resistance to AI in the business sector. Kin + Carta recently surveyed 800 leaders across the U.S. and UK and found that tech investments to accelerate change are a priority in almost every organization. But 94 percent of respondents reported *tech anxiety*, and 35 percent said they believed that AI and machine-learning technologies were moving too fast. Kin + Carta's recommendation? "Feel the fear and do it anyway."[8] The mantra is meant to be encouraging. In the remainder of the chapter, we'll show you how companies are proceeding.

OpenAI and ChatGPT

As we've discussed, AI is not new. But Conversational AI and Generative AI are finding fascinating new use cases, spurred on by creative scientists and consulting firms like Kin + Carta. One of the most important companies in this expansion has been OpenAI, an artificial intelligence research organization.

The key contribution of OpenAI has been creating an easy-to-use software application that makes AI technologies accessible to a wider range of computer users. ChatGPT was released in late 2022 and functions as a "frontend interface," allowing users to type simple sentences or questions into a text box and receive answers in the same session. The human–computer dialog is the result of AI research known as Conversational AI. There have been numerous attempts to do this in the past, but ChatGPT has taken the world by storm and is demonstrating the power of this innovation. Companies like Microsoft have announced that they are building similar technologies into search engines, like Bing, and productivity apps, like Microsoft 365 Copilot. If you think about it, though, the essential breakthrough is that it allows users to ask complex questions of computers using everyday speech. It's a usability feature based on language processing that is built on decades of AI research.

And we're talking *a lot of users*. ChatGPT is one of the most rapidly adopted technologies in the history of computers, with almost 100 million users in less than two months. Some of the most popular topics in ChatGPT sessions are computer programming, "hacking," mathematics, art and design, and concept formation. But really, the sky's the limit.

Are there any drawbacks connected to the increased use of AI?

Jeff Raikes, a former executive at Microsoft and the Bill & Melinda Gates Foundation, writes regularly about the implications of AI in business. In a September 2023 article entitled "New Tech, Old Problems: The Obstacles AI Must Overcome," Raikes highlighted some of the hidden challenges of running the *machines* that enable AI computations. One overlooked factor is the increased water usage needed to keep advanced computing systems cool in order to operate at the computational levels required to implement AI. This practical consideration reminds us that AI computing does not *actually* take place "in the cloud," but is found in increasingly complex computer centers that consume scarce resources.

Raikes is also alarmed about AI's current limitations around bias and racist content due to a lack of representative data in training samples. Essentially, human biases are making their way into AI systems because the training data reflects historical and social inequities. As a technologist, Raikes is concerned, but ultimately persuaded, that the systems will produce a net benefit, provided we facilitate rich conversations among scientists, engineers, ethicists, and social innovators. He writes:

> Ultimately, AI should improve people's lives, not make them worse. It should make workers' jobs easier and create new job opportunities. And its benefits should reach everyone, not create more inequity. If we get that right, the opportunities for positive impact are extraordinary.[9]

Witty Works: Detecting Unconscious Bias

Obviously, one of the important obligations of the tech sector is to think through potential problems related to AI and address them. Like any new system, one of the first places to shore up protocols relates to cybersecurity and the potential for harm from outside threats. However, some of the biggest vulnerabilities in companies come from inadvertent human mistakes *within* an organization.

In the case of Guardify, one of the reasons the technology scaled so quickly was not to protect the organization from outside intruders, but to limit the damage from human error within the organization or its procedures. These dangers included leaving a DVD with sensitive content unattended, or sending a restricted piece of evidence to the wrong person. Having multiple ways to ensure adherence to policy while protecting the integrity of information is often left to a company's IT department. But truly, it's everyone's responsibility to safeguard data. One social enterprise is helping frontline knowledge workers protect themselves *from themselves* in a new way.

Meet Witty Works, a small social business based in Switzerland with a cute name and a big goal. Witty Works is led by CEO and co-founder Nadia Fischer, who is hard at work to "scale inclusion faster with language," as their website advertises (https://witty.works). Nadia is not a traditional technologist. She worked in the defense department in Geneva after studying international relations with aspirations of becoming a war journalist. After being frustrated with the slow pace of government, Nadia hopped the fence to the private sector, eventually landing inside a product development team. Unfortunately, she didn't see a lot of others who looked like her, and she worried about the lack of diversity in tech.

Like all social innovators, Nadia was inspired to do something about it. Nadia founded Witty Works. Instead of just coaching women to enter the technology industry, she and her co-founder, Valérie Vuillerat, set out to change corporate culture. After some research, they discovered that unconscious bias is one of the root causes of discrimination, including stereotypes about age, gender, ethnic background, religious beliefs, and cultural values. In the business world, they saw this play out in many job advertisements, where they claim 70 percent are still written in a way that only attracts male applicants.

Witty Works created a way to help companies avoid words and phrases that might offend, exclude, or inadvertently demean others—including those already marginalized—using a software tool called "Diversifier." An example of this scenario could be a person using the words "digital natives" or "blacklist" in a business setting, not recognizing the potential for inadvertent ageism or racism.

The Witty Works technology is an AI-based language assistant that reads email and other compositions in real time, applying a suggested replacement text along with a resource to help the author consider options and train their inclusion muscle. Because Witty Works is a cloud-based AI application, data is quantified and examined to produce insights to help the organization understand areas for improvement, and realize a social return on investment (SROI) immediately. The company believes that each positive substitution made equates to error reduction in communication. In addition, the company is discovering a benefit they did not originally account for in their social innovation plan. They have been able to attribute the use of Witty Works to increased employee loyalty in companies, with increased loyalty rates up to 35 percent.

Witty Works is a communication enhancer centered on four use cases: HR, People and Culture; Marketing and Communications;

Recruiting; and C-Level Communication. However, users don't have to work at an enterprise-level organization to benefit from this type of coaching. It's free for anyone to use through a simple web browser extension.

The Witty Works pricing model currently has three tiers: Witty Free, Witty Teams (with a startup/NGO discount up to 50%), and Witty Enterprise, with pricing and features for larger organizations. On the business side, Witty Works is adhering to a few of our recommended strategies for partnering and product development. They are currently developing a Microsoft Word add-in to utilize the low-cost infrastructure of Microsoft 365, bringing their inclusive language model to millions of potential customers.

I, Robot?

Now let's address the elephant in the living room. This chapter was not written by AI, but parts of it could have been. Although tempting, we never intended to use AI for content generation in this book, nor was it used for any of our text or artwork. Interestingly, our publisher even has a thoughtful policy around AI that we consulted from time to time while preparing our content for this book. Social impact organizations should follow suit, developing guidelines related to AI usage and content creation. If you don't have one already, it is something to put on your to-do list so that employees and stakeholders have some clarity as you navigate the ethical and practical considerations related to AI. It will help you stay competitive, avoid copyright infringement, and use your human resources in ways that are uniquely human.

Career Training for Social Impact

Harnessing AI for the public interest is something Shelly and her team at Giving Tech Labs started to explore in earnest starting in 2019. Led by Dr. Ying Li, Chief Scientist, the team began to consider how artificial intelligence could be used to serve the public interest. The work included the training and development of junior data scientists as AI fellows. The lab hoped to create new tools and approaches for evaluating existing datasets, supporting *informatics* around the United Nations Sustainable Development Goals (UN SDGs) and other *success measures* within nonprofits and philanthropies. The University of Washington, where many of the AI fellows hailed from, describes informatics as "the study, design, and development of information technology for the good of people, organizations, and society."[10] Under the leadership of Dr. Ying

Li, a world-renowned data scientist, Giving Tech Labs created the program to expose fellows to the application of AI to problems in the social impact sector.

In 18 months, Dr. Ying graduated ten research fellows and published three research papers in AI-related publications, including "Domain-Specific Knowledge Graph as a Public Service," published by Knowledge Discovery and Data Mining (KDD), a special interest group of the Association for Computing Machinery (ACM).[11] The acceptance rate for Dr. Ying's program was low and the bar was high. But those who were accepted were part of a research team using "edge computing" strategies to bring computation and data storage closer to the sources of data. They also used AI to turn massive amounts of information into insights that could advance the team's understanding of large-scale, complex problems. For Dr. Ying, a problem is only worth solving if it's a hard problem. During Dr. Ying's time at Giving Tech Labs, OpenAI's consumer-facing technology had not yet been released. The team worked tirelessly to build, test, report, and improve the accuracy of their AI-based systems. Projects included analyzing data and trends related to older Americans and finding patterns when evaluating impact-driven philanthropy by UN SDG. They also developed AI-driven speech analysis tools, without compromising on personal privacy for users.

Shelly's experience at Giving Tech Labs shows how rapidly AI has changed the social impact landscape. At the high end, AI research is engaging the minds of the most proficient computer scientists in the field. Career training in artificial intelligence, data science, data mining, and data analytics are among the most sought-after programs in colleges and universities. One of the challenges is training AI practitioners at scale, including entry-level employees who have basic statistical knowledge, data entry skills, some programming experience, and the ability to present data effectively in teams.[12] We are particularly inspired by Polly Allen, a former technical manager on the Amazon Alexa project who founded a company called AI Career Boost.[13] Allen's belief is that anyone can be a part of the AI Revolution, not just those with advanced training or coding abilities. The demand for AI technology can also be turned into a pathway for meaningful employment.

Fostering Trust

Depending on who you ask, you will get vastly different definitions about what AI really is, based on the experiences and acumen of the respondent. Dave Gilson, from Stanford University's Graduate

School of Business, aptly notes, "AI has become a shorthand for everything from generative tools like ChatGPT and machine learning to computer vision and robotic process automation."[14] His conversations with fellow professors helped him to articulate how organizations should deploy AI "nimbly, strategically and responsibly," which is a helpful framework for how social impact organizations might think about their approach. Of course, this is a roadmap for the *how* but not the *why* of deploying AI strategies.

At the 2023 Concordia Annual Summit in New York City, a session entitled "The Nexus of AI and Misinformation" connected the topics of purpose and impact to AI technologies. In the session, Reggie Townsend, Vice President of Data Ethics Practice at SAS, described AI as a *lifecycle*. Rather than considering AI to be a service or a feature of a product, he reminded the audience that AI involves a set of *algorithmic techniques* that are not new. Amazon's Alexa, Uber, and other commonly used applications are powered by AI. Today's conversations in board rooms and senate chambers are not necessarily focused on *if* AI should be used, but on *how* to use it responsibly. Reggie made the case that Responsible AI has to include responsible rhetoric, not slogans or warnings that panic people.

Organizations using AI should get back to the potential *benefits* of these systems, and focus on building trust and adoption, instead of fear-mongering. Shelly saw this first-hand in a recent meeting, where a nonprofit executive anxiously asked, "Our website won't have AI in it, will it?" The reaction is common, imagining AI as a kind of poison pill or Trojan horse sent to harm consumers and destroy the organizations that adopt it. The reality is that AI, like many previous technologies, brings with it the kind of anxiety usually associated with political or religious reform. Something similar took place during the introduction of textile machinery, automobiles, airplanes, and birth control pills. Organizations that were founded or flourished prior to the AI revolution are often skeptical or alarmed at the idea that AI can automate routine tasks, support complex decision making, and create new value in organizations.

Arizona State University's President Michael Crow simply argues that *resistance is futile*.[15] According to Crow, we are at a moment in history in which we are building tools for human enhancement, complexity management, and decision making. We need to proceed with caution. But there are almost boundless possibilities in store due to the power of AI. There are also grave problems that need to be acknowledged.

For example, Yalda Aokar, an advisor to policy makers on digital development, reports that child sexual assault material (CSAM) has increased tenfold in the last decade.[16] With the rapid development of AI has come the normalizing of sexual assault and other anti-social behaviors, in contexts that in previous times would be hard to imagine. Yalda raises awareness about this troubling trend to show that "deep fakes" that depict sexual assault don't necessarily need to be grounded in reality. AI has the ability to construct images for art, entertainment, or abuse that are not real, though they break social and ethical guidelines. Law enforcement officers who are charged to detect, protect, and prosecute digital criminals are often left in a complex world of outdated regulations and complex computing tools.

This is a reminder that AI and distributed computing has its dark side. For this reason, technological innovation often needs limits, regulation, and transparency in how it is used.

A Perspective from an AI Luminary

Igor Jablokov is a pioneer in the field of artificial intelligence. He founded Pyron and Yap, the latter being the world's first automated cloud platform with accurate voice recognition. Yap became Amazon's first AI-related acquisition. Without his efforts, we might not have Alexa, Echo, or Fire TV. When he worked at IBM, Igor was responsible for the early version of Watson, the conversational computing system that could understand a person's natural language, instead of just computer coding. Igor is an innovator in human language technologies and uses his position for good. He is passionate about fostering career and educational opportunities for others entering the fields of science, technology, engineering, and math (STEM).

According to Igor, AI didn't start with a plot for total world domination. It started to help accessibility and language gaps. It was originally created as a pathway for social progress, to remove barriers for people with disabilities. AI can truly be considered a piece of social impact history. In Chapter 4, we featured three innovative companies that have also addressed this space, including Voiceitt, Ability Central, and No Limbits. The technologies that these innovators have developed are transformative for people with disabilities. Igor believed that AI would enable this work for generations. He was just as surprised as anyone to see the dark side of AI emerge because of bad actors.

"The web as we know it died last year as an expression of human creativity," Igor declared from the Concordia Annual Summit stage in late 2023.[17] The inventor believes that by 2030, the vast majority of the content on the world wide web will be generative. At the conference session, a discussion took shape about creating a seed bank of truth because it is becoming increasingly difficult to discern fake news and misinformation from fact and truth. Igor likened the problem to a person's journey escaping a hall of mirrors. Ending his presentation on a dour note, he announced that social media is providing a low-cost infrastructure to enable ill-intent.

AI Integration with Nonprofits

We'd like to raise up a different vision, the insights of Luis Salazar, the founder and CEO of AI4SP (https://ai4sp.org), an organization that creates, uses, supports, and invests in AI that works for all. Luis sees the rise of AI as the Fourth Industrial Revolution, noting that the adoption of AI is happening much faster than the adoption of electricity, the PC, or the Internet.[18]

To contextualize this social and technological shift, Luis notes that over half of American adults have a literacy rate below the sixth grade. In the U.S., 40 million adults read below third-grade level.[19] The rapid speed of transformation combined with low literacy rates presents a challenge to integrate millions of Americans into the AI digital economy. Beyond reading, writing, and critical-thinking skills, the workplace requires many workers to use email, word processors, spreadsheets, and data-related tools. Others need to create and manage digital content, collaborate with others, and develop conceptual skills in cybersecurity, privacy, and data compliance. The danger is that many workers will be left behind if they don't fill skill gaps and receive appropriate training.

On the positive side, however, there is hope that AI-powered tools can help with both skill assessment and skill delivery. New learning programs can be scalable, assessable, and designed to help a range of learners adapt to changing landscapes. The opportunity exists for AI tools to drive economic advancement and personal growth in the evolving digital economy, even if many jobs change during the process.

In addition to skilling challenges, there will be ethical dilemmas. AI4SP highlights the complex ethical problems that will arise if AI-powered systems are allowed to perpetuate biases in healthcare, housing, tenant approval, mortgage qualifications, and hiring practices.

Even big business has made missteps in this regard. At Amazon, for example, a recruiting tool powered by machine learning was shuttered because it routinely excluded or downgraded female candidates in the applicant pool.[20]

What should conscientious organizations do to move forward? Commissioned by Microsoft, AI4SP has developed a series of useful AI integration guidelines for nonprofits entitled "Navigating AI Integration: 7 Steps for Nonprofits."[21] We summarize the list below. We recommend the resource as a self-assessment tool for all leaders in the social impact sector, especially those who are considering AI as a way to enhance operations or service customers.

Follow These Step to Integrate AI into Your Organization

- **Step 1: Awareness and Education**—Explore AI use cases and see how AI can be applied to your operations.
- **Step 2: Spot AI Potential and Assess Readiness**—Select a pilot use case for AI, focusing on areas like automation, fundraising, community engagement, or impact analytics.
- **Step 3: Choose AI Tools and Test them with Safe Data**—Evaluate the best tools for your organization and test them with a non-sensitive "testing" dataset.
- **Step 4: Security, Compliance, Privacy, and Ethics**—Consider legal regulations, examine potential biases, and review ethical considerations related to the tools you've selected.
- **Step 5: Implement AI Pilots**—Craft a detailed rollout strategy with key dates and milestones.
- **Step 6: Monitor AI Performance**—Establish clear KPIs and gather feedback from customers, donors, and team members.
- **Step 7: Ongoing Enhancement and Oversight of AI in Your Tech**—Evaluate all AI tools regularly, share outcomes with stakeholders, and keep abreast of new opportunities.

The benefit of following this process is that it allows organizations to explore, select, pilot, share, and evaluate AI technologies through a series of discrete steps that build momentum. Implementing AI is not simply "flipping a switch," but a series of business decisions that align well with normal strategic planning tasks and digital transformation. At the heart of this process is innovating for the public good.

Biomonitoring with Bees

Do you remember Shelly's 94-year-old grandfather mentioned in Chapter 6? Ed Weber was born in Montana as the son of a Norwegian immigrant, and he spent his whole life connected to farming and land management in some way. When Shelly was a child, he worked for the Oregon Department of Soil Conversation and would often talk about collecting samples along the Klamath River that flowed through Oregon.

Today, that same land is being monitored for pollution by honey bees through a tool called BeeOmonitoring, a system using machine learning and artificial intelligence to extrapolate data over large areas to assess environmental impact factors. Did you know that a colony of bees can collect pollen samples from 4 billion different plants in just one year?

The system was developed by BeeOdiversity, founded in 2012 by three unlikely Belgian founders, Dr. Bach Kim Nguyen, Michaël van Cutsem, and Emmanuel Lion. The three were brought together by their shared interest in protecting bees and their ecosystems. The "BeeOmonitoring" (also known as biomonitoring) analyzes pollen collected by bees that act as natural drones. The data is stored in the cloud through Azure Data Factory, Microsoft's cloud service for data integration, which is used to identify more than 500 pesticides.[22]

In doing so, bees are helping scientists and ecologists develop nature-based solutions, developing the model for future biodiversity and clean air initiatives. The information gathered through this AI-powered technology allows for targeted action by communicating with the local community, developing evaluation criteria, and informing interventions to increase the number and type of plant diversity in the ecosystem. It also provides qualitative and quantitative data based on pollution. The company prides itself on its fruitful collaboration, drawing on "the brilliance of Mother Nature, on technological innovation and on the involvement of all the stakeholders in a project."[23] The data collected by the BeeOdiversity team is now being used by private companies to report on their environmental, social, and governance (ESG) initiatives.

Jean-Philippe Courtois is Microsoft's Executive Vice President and President, National Transformation Partnerships. He is also the executive sponsor of the "Entrepreneurship for Positive Impact" program, where BeeOdiversity is joined by over 1,000 changemakers across 70 countries. The program seeks to connect shared goals, to solve for common pain points across multiple corporate structures, from social entrepreneurs to social impact startups. Jean-Philippe believes that AI will ultimately transform every country, every industry, every workplace, and all our lives. He is an optimist and believes that AI can truly transform the world for good. At the 2023 United Nations General Assembly in New York City, Jean-Philippe noted, "AI innovation provides new ways to make real progress towards the UN SDGs and will ultimately support the creation of sustainable and inclusive economies."[24]

Jean-Philippe is not just a passionate champion for innovation and impact; he understands what it's like to "walk the talk." He is a Frenchman with a heart for impact and a head for business. His Microsoft career spans over 40 years. And yet, in 2015, along with his family, he started Live for Good, a charitable foundation designed to help young people realize their full potential through social entrepreneurship and digital innovation. Jean-Philippe thought big but started small—our book's theme. You can find inspiration through his example at www.live-for-good.org.

The Big Picture

Neil deGrasse Tyson helped popularize scientific research and brought an exciting context to human existence. When he was still in graduate school, he studied how stars and galaxies form and evolve over time. Tyson helped us understand how the universe functions. He is also famous for reminding us, "We are part of this universe; we are in this universe, but perhaps more important than both of those facts, is that the universe is in us."[25]

As one species, we need to work against organizing ourselves, our work, and our problems into silos, sorted by sector. We need an interdisciplinary approach and a convergence model to shape our work on Earth, where our purpose is shared and our methods are inclusive and sustainable. We can create innovative solutions through catalytic approaches to spark positive social innovation at scale. We hope the examples and experiences we shared in *This Little World* clearly show how that work can be accomplished.

This is just the beginning of a movement in which social and environmental challenges are addressed, economic growth is inclusive, and the fundamental rights of people are supported through empathy and creativity. What's next remains to be seen. But we believe the future is bright for this little world. There is a thriving, flourishing, dynamic community of changemakers working across sectors to make meaningful contributions to our planet and its creatures.

Please join the movement, and bring others along with you!

We'll close with a quote from the British journalist and TV host Jeremy Clarkson, who often covers motorsports like Formula One. Clarkson reminds us, "Speed has never killed anyone. Suddenly becoming stationary, that's what gets you."[26] So go forth and innovate. With the wind at your back and limitless possibilities ahead, don't stop until you reach your destination.

This little world is counting on you.

Notes

1   For the Y2K controversy, see Michael Halvorson and Michael Young, *Running Microsoft Office 2000* (Redmond, WA: Microsoft Press, May 1999), p. xxxix. For Halvorson's quote and a popular version of the story, see "Year 2000 Problem," Wikipedia, last modified December 10, 2023, https://en.wikipedia.org/wiki/Year_2000_problem.

2   To read more about how technology mirrors culture and society, see Thomas J. Misa, *Leonardo to the Internet: Technology and Culture from the Renaissance to the Present,* Third Edition (Baltimore, MD: The Johns Hopkins University Press, 2022); and *Does Technology Drive History? The Dilemma of Technological Determinism,* eds. Merritt Roe Smith and Leo Marx (Cambridge, MA: The MIT Press, 1994).

3   Brad Smith and Carol Ann Browne, *Tools and Weapons: The Promise and the Peril of the Digital Age,* Updated Edition (New York: Penguin, 2021).

4   Among the many fascinating works, see *Artificial Intelligence for Business Creativity,* edited by Margherita Pagani and Renaud Champion (London: Routledge, 2024); Kenneth Wenger, *Is the Algorithm Working Against Us? A Layperson's Guide to the Concepts, Math, and Pitfalls of AI* (New York: Working Fires Foundation, 2023); Ajay Agrawal, Joshua Gans, and Avi Goldfarb, *Prediction Machines, Updated and Expanded: The Simple Economics of Artificial Intelligence* (Cambridge, MA: Harvard Business Review, 2022); Henry Kissinger, Eric Schmidt, and Daniel Huttenlocher, *The Age of AI* (New York: Back Bay Books, 2022); Kai-Fu Lee, *AI Superpowers: China, Silicon Valley and the New World Order* (New York: Harper Business, 2021); *Possible Minds: Twenty-Five Ways of Looking at AI,* edited by John Brockman (London: Penguin Press, 2020); and James Lovelock with Bryan Appleyard, *Novacene: The Coming Age of Hyperintelligence* (Cambridge, MA: The MIT Press, 2020).

5   Brad Darrach, "Meet Shaky, the First Electronic Person," *Life* (November 20, 1970), 58B.

6   The PEAK grantmaking session took place on June 29, 2023. For the details, see www.peakgrantmaking.org/resource/ai-for-good-revolutionizing-philanthropy-with-innovative-solutions-fluxx/. Accessed December 10, 2023.

7   Paul Daugherty, Bhaskar Ghosh, Karthik Narain, Lan Guan, and Jim Wilson, "AI for Everyone," *Accenture* (March 23, 2023). www.accenture.com/us-en/insights/technology/generative-ai. Accessed December 10, 2023.

8   Kin + Carta, "2024 Leadership Priorities in Tech: Leading through Tech Anxiety" (London, 2023), 10–11. https://ssir.org/articles/entry/rediscovering_social_innovation. Accessed December 10, 2023.

9   Jeff Raikes, "New Tech, Old Problems: The Obstacles AI Must Overcome," Forbes (September 27, 2023). www.forbes.com/sites/jeffraikes/2023/09/27/new-tech-old-problems-the-obstacles-ai-must-overcome. Accessed December 10, 2023.

10 To learn about the University of Washington Informatics program, visit https://ischool.uw.edu/programs/informatics/what-is-informatics.

11 Ying Li, Vitalii Zakhozhyi, Daniel Zhu, and Luis Salazar, "Domain-Specific Knowledge Graph as a Public Service: Powering Social Impact Funding in the US," *KDD '20: Proceedings of the 26th*

ACM SIGKDD International Conference on Knowledge Discovery & Data Mining (New York: ACM, 2020). https://dl.acm.org/doi/abs/10.1145/3394486.3403330. Accessed December 10, 2023.

12 Data.org, "Workforce Wanted: Data Talent for Social Impact" (2022), 26. https://data.org/reports/workforce-wanted/. Accessed December 10, 2023.

13 For more information about AI Career Boost and its mission and curriculum, visit www.aicareerboost.com.

14 Dave Gilson, "Is your Business Ready to Jump into AI? Read This First." *Stanford Social Innovation Review* (October 25, 2023). www.gsb.stanford.edu/insights/your-business-ready-jump-ai-read-first. Accessed December 10, 2023.

15 Michael Crow, "The Nexus of Artificial Intelligence (AI) and Misinformation," Concordia Annual Summit session, September 18, 2023.

16 Yalda Aokar, "The Nexus of Artificial Intelligence (AI) and Misinformation," Concordia Annual Summit session, September 18, 2023.

17 Igor Jablokov, "The Nexus of Artificial Intelligence (AI) and Misinformation," Concordia Annual Summit session, September 18, 2023.

18 For perceptive insights about AI and digital transformation, see https://ai4sp.org/ai-insights-and-reports/. Accessed April 7, 2024.

19 For adult literacy data, see https://nces.ed.gov/pubs2019/2019179/index.asp. Accessed April 7, 2024.

20 For the news story as reported by the Carnegie Mellon University School of Computer Science, see www.ml.cmu.edu/news/news-archive/2016-2020/2018/october/amazon-scraps-secret-artificial-intelligence-recruiting-engine-that-showed-biases-against-women.html. Accessed December 10, 2023.

21 https://ai4sp.org/wp-content/uploads/2023/10/7-steps-to-AI-Adoption-Nonprofits-Fall-2023.pdf. Accessed April 7, 2024.

22 Chris Welsch, "Assisted by AI, a workforce of bees tracks pollution and boosts biodiversity," September 18, 2023. https://news.microsoft.com/source/emea/features/assisted-by-ai-a-workforce-of-bees-tracks-pollution-and-boosts-biodiversity/. Accessed December 10, 2023.

23 For this quote and other resources, see https://beeodiversity.com. Accessed December 10, 2023.

24 Jean-Philippe Courtois, United Nations General Assembly (New York, NY), September 19, 2023.

25 Neil deGrasse Tyson, "How Neil deGrasse Tyson would Save the World," *Time Magazine's Ten Questions*, June 27, 2008. Available on YouTube beginning at 3:35, www.youtube.com/watch?v=wiOwqDmacJo. Accessed December 10, 2023.

26 Jeremy Clarkson, *Top Gear*, Series 10, Episode 6 (November 18, 2007).

About the Authors

Michael Halvorson, Ph.D., is a professor of business history and innovation who writes and teaches about digital transformation and public interest technology. He was an early employee at Microsoft, contributing to the development of Microsoft Press, Visual Studio, and Microsoft Office. He is currently Director of Innovation Studies and Benson Family Chair of Business and Economic History at Pacific Lutheran University. Michael is the author of 40 books about history and technology, and he served for ten years as an executive leader at Compass Housing Alliance, a social impact organization in Seattle. Research and publication data at https://orcid.org/0000-0001-9171-4380.

Shelly Cano Kurtz is a social entrepreneur and consultant who has founded numerous social innovation organizations and initiatives, including a social impact incubator, an evidence management solution for nonprofits and government agencies, and a data insights platform for entrepreneurs who are creating public interest technology. She is also an advisor for Concordia, a bi-partisan organization dedicated to building cross-sector partnerships, and the Center for Workforce Inclusion, a nonprofit focused on workforce development for older Americans. Shelly has been involved in over 200 go-to-market campaigns and regularly serves as a mentor for social innovators in the U.S.

Index

Ability Central 54–56
achievement gap 99
Agile methodology 19, 39, 44n3, 59, 88, 91
AI for Good (movement) 148–51
AI4SP 159–60
airplanes 16
Amazon Alexa 47, 50–51, 156–58
Amazon Web Services (AWS) 24, 121
Ambachew, Heven *116*
Americans with Disabilities Act (ADA) 56
Aokar, Yalda 157
Apple: iPad 41; iPhone 41, 48–50, 69; Watch 41; Siri 47, 50–51; Store 41
Arabic 10
artificial intelligence (AI): biased content 153–55; ChatGPT 152–53, 157; Conversational 147, 149, 152, 158; Generative 147, 149, 152, 157–58; gig economy tools 40–42; 'for good' movement 148–52; history of research 149; ideation without 78; misinformation 157; and nonprofits 156–57; OpenAI 152; recommended reading 163n4; in speech recognition 51; structured data for 113, 118; tech for good jobs 11; training practitioners 156
Artime, Michael 80
Ashoka 12n3, 126
Australia 17

autism spectrum 53–55
Ayoub, Tarek 7–11

Badshah, Aktar 62
BeeOdiversity 160–62
beta version 83
Bill & Melinda Gates Foundation 5, 142–43, 145n18, 153
Bing 152
Blackbaud (company) 114, 118
Blockbuster (company) 105
Blue Zones Project 117
Boyd, Sara 31–33
brainstorming *see* Ideation stage
Brazil 10
Broadband Telecom (company) 127
Brown, Dr. Maoz 89
Brown, Tim 64
Browne, Carol Ann 149
Bruce, Afua 113
Brussels 10
business ethics *see* ethics
business-to-business (B2B) model 20, 109, 134

Campbell, Mary *116*
Canada 17
carbon sequestration *see* Forestmatic
catalytic philanthropy 143, 145n20
Center for Workforce Inclusion (CWI) 4, 102–104
change management 35
changemaking 2–3, 10, 14, 18, 64

ChatGPT 41–42, 51, 144, 152–53, 157
Cherry, Matt 53–56
cholera 15
citizenship 4, 80–81, 85
civic engagement (case study) 79–85
Civil war 16, 142
Clarkson, Jeremy 162
climate change 2, 7–10, 13–14, 20–22, 108, 119
cloud computing 19, 33, 43, 109, 121, 141, 150
Code.org (organization) 41, 67, 86n4
Cole, Erica 57–60
collective impact 6, 96, 117, 134
Compass Housing Alliance 17
compassion (defined) 48
computer programming 44n4
Concordia 4, 157–58
confirmation bias 111
constraints 65–66
Conversational AI 149, 152
Courtois, Jean-Philippe 161
Covid-19 22–23, 38, 43n2, 59, 84, 136, 143
cross-subsidization model 135
Crow, Michael 157
CSS 10
Cuban, Mark 58, 60
Curmà, Mattia 7–11
customer relationship management (CRM) 113
cybersecurity 150, 153, 159

data: analytics 155–56; collection 87, 107, 112–14; conditions for scaling 131–33, 140; dashboard 9, 109, *110*, 115–16, 121, *122*; dictionary 115; and digital transformation 141; gathering 100, 108, 114, 118, 123, 133; measuring impact with 114–17; models for nonprofits 118–19; security 113; for social impact 107–12

database 111–15
dataset 115, 160
Define stage (design) 73–77
deGrasse Tyson, Neil 162
design thinking: curriculum at PLU 65; defined 63–66; five stages 86; journey map 79; process 64–66; sequential diagram 68; Venn diagram 66
diffusion of technical skills 44n4
digital readiness *see* digital transformation
digital transformation: checklist for self-assessment 36–38; defined 29–30; goal in a social impact organization 35; low-cost infrastructures 40–43; pace of 38–40; and scaling 141–42; and UN SDGs 23
digital-first principles 37–41
digitalization *see* digital transformation
disability: clothing design 58–59; compassion crisis 53; deaf and hard of hearing 56; definition 52–53; intersectional with UN SDGs 53; speech 47–50
Disability Opportunity Fund 52, 58
disruption 130–31
diversity and inclusion 67, 115, 150
Drayton, Bill 126

Earth: fragile nature of 2; humanity-first principles 151; largest country (India) 69; plan of UN SDGs 20; population 13; summary of innovation principles 162
economies of scale *see* scaling
ecosystem 87, 91
Eguillor, Marcos 8–9
empathy (defined) 47–49, 95–96
Empathy stage (design) 68–73, 81
enterprise resource planning (ERP) 35, 40

Equal Opportunity Schools (EOS) 98–100
ethics: in AI 149–50, 155, 158–60; in data collection 95; in digital transformation 40; in mission statement 61; principles 95; responsible business practices 138, 157; scaling innovations 137

Facebook 41
fee-for-service (model) 135
Fischer, Nadia 154
Footprint (company) 133
forensic interviews 30
Forestmatic (company) 7–11, 108–10, 123
franchises 127
French (language) 10

Generation Z 1
Generative AI 149, 152
gig economy 42
Gilson, Dave 157
Giving Compass (organization) 24–25, 91, 107
Giving Compass Insights see X4i.org
Giving Tech Labs (organization) 24, 31–32, 155–56
global challenges (summary of) 14
Google Apps 129–30
Google Workplace 40–42
Gordon, Robert J. 16
Grede, Emma 58, 60
Green solutions 10
gross domestic product (GDP) 16, 18, 136
Guardify (company) 30–36, 43, 119–22, 153

Halvorson, Felix 116
Hammerman, Charles 58
Healthcare sector 17, 42, 46–51, 54, 59, 64–65, 113, 127, 132, 135–36, 142–43

Hidden Figures (film) 165
hiking trails 42
history of technology (methodology) 6, 15–18, 148
HTML 10
human-centered design (HCD) 5, 19, 63–64, 72, 85n2, 86n9, 139

Ideation stage (design) 77–82
IDEO (organization) 63–64, 68–69, 78, 85n2
ikigai 96–98
impact entrepreneurs 6
indoor plumbing 15–16
innovation curriculum 70–72, 74
Innovation Studies (program) 4–5, 65, 79, 115
The Innovator's Dilemma (book) 130
iOS (operating system) 48, 69
IRS data 24, 132

Jablokov, Igor 158
Jackson, Ben 33
Japan 17
Jeff Raikes 142–43, 153
journey map see design thinking
just-in-time approach 92

Kardashian, Khloé 60
Kelly, Tom 69–70
key performance indicators (KPIs) 3, 95, 107, 116–17, 120, 160
Kickstarter campaign 58
Kin + Carta (company) 151–52
Koehler, Susan 88, 101–102, 133

Lebanon 10
LGBTQ+ groups 26
Li, Ying 23–24, 155–56
LinkedIn 3, 6
logframes 119
Lutheran higher education 4, 65
Lutheran Sailors and Loggers Mission (organization) 17

Madrid 7
makerspaces 74
market landscape analysis 90–91,
    131
McDonald's (company)
    111–12
McGuinness, Tara Dawson 123
measles 15
Mexico City 10
Microsoft 365 40–42
Microsoft Corporation: Azure
    Data Factory 161; common
    data model 117–19; company
    mission 1; Copilot (product)
    152; Dynamics 365 (product)
    35, 114, 118; Excel (product)
    114, 129; Office (product) 4,
    129, 163n1; skilling 11; Teams
    (product) 40; Tech for Social
    Impact 19; Windows (product)
    41; Word (product) 129, 155
Microsoft Press 4
Millennials 1
Minecraft 41
minimum viable product (MVP)
    83, 88, 91–94, 114–16
Minsky, Marvin 149
mission statements 45–46, 62n12,
    87, 96, 138

Nadella, Satya 1
National Institutes of Health
    (NIH) 140
Nebraska 31, 35
Netflix 105
No Limbits 57–60
Nonprofit sector: AI integration
    159; common data model for
    118; history of 17–18; IRS data
    132; organizations 5; size in U.S.
    18; support for 55; tech for PI
    movement 94

Officer, Gary 103–104
Open Data for Social Impact
    (framework) 119
OpenAI (organization) 152

opportunity gap 99
outcomes: at Equal Opportunity
    Schools 99, 103; to evaluate
    AI tools 160; at Guardify 31;
    for marginalized groups 26;
    showing progress 93; test before
    scaling 131; theory of change
    87–89, 132

Pacific Lutheran University (PLU)
    4, 65, 79–81, 114–16
Pareto Principle see scaling: 80/20
    rule
partnerships 21, 52, 98, 109, 126,
    142–44, 161
Peabody Education Fund 18
PEAK grantmaking 89
Peshock, Anna 59
pesticides 161
philanthropy 18, 56; see also
    catalytic philanthropy
Phoenix Suns 134
podcast 41
point-of-sale system 36
pollen 161
Portugal 10
problem statement (defining) 73–77
Project Harmony (organization)
    31–32
prosthetics 59
Prototype stage (design) 3, 9, 24,
    82–85, 92, 139
public health 16
public interest technology 14–15,
    37, 123
purpose-driven organizations
    45–46
Python 10

rabies 15
radio 15
rainwater harvesting (Senegal)
    72–73
Red Cross 18
reforestation 7–9
Regan, Ronald 150
relational map 79

replication *see* scaling
Responsible AI 150
return on investment (ROI) 3, 35, 37, 109; *see also* social return on investment
Richard II (play) 2

Salazar, Luis 23, 103, 159–60
Salesforce (company) 114, 118
Salvation Army 18
scaling: 80/20 rule 128–30; Bill & Melinda Gates Foundation 142–44; creative partnerships 142–44; defined 19, 125–28; digital readiness 141–42; disruptive innovation 130–31; environmental sustainability 137–38; economic conditions needed 135–36; essential conditions for 131; Forestmatic case study 10; malaria case study 142–44; reducing unit cost 136–37; tech for good organizations 19
Scandinavia 17
Schank, Hana 123
schema (data) 118–19
scientific research 15–18, 119, 133, 162
service deserts 23, 131–32
Shakespeare, William 2
shared pain point 37
Shark Tank 57–60
Simon Sinek *see* Start with Why
single-use plastics 133–34
skilling 11, 67
smallpox 15
SMART (guideline) 114
smartphone 41
Smith, Brad 149
Smolley, Sara 49–50
social entrepreneurs 3, 6, 12n4, 23, 126–27
social entrepreneurship contests 49
social impact sector: defined 3, 18; origins 26; size of U.S. marketplace 13

social media 42
social return on investment (SROI) 109–12, 128, 154
software-as-a-service (SaaS) model 32, 34, 37, 111, 134
South Sound Together (organization) 79–80, 84–85
Spain 10
Special Olympics 5
Standard of living index 15–17
Stanford University 156
Start with Why 56–57
Stockbauer, Todd 60
success metrics 33, 107–13, 123, 140
sustainability 7, 10–11, 42, 64, 95, 101–102, 109, 112, 134, 138

teaming (defined) 71–72
tech for good 3–6, 19–20; Agile methods 39; and AI 148–49; characteristics of organizations 20; cloud computing 141; design thinking for 68; featured in X4i.org 24; Forestmatic 10–12; Guardify 29, 33, 121; movement characteristics 6, 19–20; revenue model 134; scaling 127; social return on investment 111; technology for the public interest 94–95; Voiceitt 52
Tech4PI 94–96, 98
technological innovation (shortcomings) 6, 17–19, 26, 148–49, 158
telegraph 15
Test stage (design) 82–85, 88, 91–94, 139, 143, 160
theory of action *100*
theory of change 83, 87–91, 99–105, 109, 127–28, 132–33, 140–41
TikTok 41
Tiomkin, Stas 48
Townsend, Reggie 157
Toyama, Kentaro 6
tree planting *see* Forestmatic

tuberculosis 15
Turner, Cameron 152

United Nations Sustainable
Development Goals (UN SDGs):
Clean Water and Sanitation
73; Climate Action 8; Decent
Work and Economic Growth
26; defined 20–21; global
market size 11; Good Health
and Well-being 26; Life on Land
8; list of 21–22; No Poverty
22, 25–26; Peace, Justice, and
Strong Institutions 32–33;
Quality Education 26; Reduced
Inequality 26; Sustainable Cities
26, 127; Zero Hunger 45
United Way (organization) 18,
45, 127

value proposition 93
Verresen, Alexander 7–11
VidaNyx see Guardify
vocation: advancing the public
good 7; and ikigai 97;

Innovation Studies (PLU)
65; Matt Cherry's story 54;
personal theory of change 101;
purpose-drive work 46; Susan
Koehler's story 101–102; see
also Lutheran higher education
Voiceitt (company) 49–52

Ward, Amy Sample 113
Weber, Ed 90
Weiss, Carol 104
Weissberg, Danny 46–49
Western Europe 17
Wi-Fi 42, 127
Witty Works (organization)
153–55
World Bank 18

X4i.org (organization) 6, 8, 24–25,
55, 91, 144n10

YMCA 18, 125, 140
Y2K problem 148

Zoom (product) 3, 40

Printed in the United States
by Baker & Taylor Publisher Services